BRAIN HEALTH PUZZLES FOR ADULTS

CROSSWORDS, SUDOKU, AND OTHER PUZZLES THAT GIVE THE BRAIN THE EXERCISE IT NEEDS

PHIL FRAAS

Andrews McMeel
PUBLISHING®

Andrews McMeel Publishing
a division of Andrews McMeel Universal
1130 Walnut Street, Kansas City, Missouri 64106

www.andrewsmcmeel.com

23 24 25 26 27 MCN 10 9 8 7 6 5 4 3 2 1

ISBN: 978-1-5248-8049-1

Editor: Patty Rice
Art Director: Julie Barnes
Production Editor: Elizabeth A. Garcia
Production Manager: Chadd Keim

ATTENTION: SCHOOLS AND BUSINESSES
Andrews McMeel books are available at quantity discounts with bulk purchase for educational, business, or sales promotional use. For information, please e-mail the Andrews McMeel Publishing Special Sales Department: sales@amuniversal.com.

INTRODUCTION

Many adults have come to realize that keeping their brains healthy is an important part of their lives, just like keeping in good physical shape. And, for the more mature among us, there is the added interest in taking proactive steps to stave off a decline in cognitive fitness as we age. The good news is that science tells us that adult brain health can be protected and enhanced by several things, including maintaining our physical health, following a good diet, getting adequate rest, engaging in socialization, and keeping the mind active with puzzles and games to enhance cognitive fitness.

While the research is still ongoing, studies have shown that brain exercise, including working on puzzles, can do much to improve our cognitive fitness. Studies that focused on puzzle-solving have found benefits such as improved attention, memory, and reasoning for a study group of crossword and Sudoku fans and improved pattern recognition skills associated with working on puzzles.

To be sure, there is no definitive answer to the question of which brain exercises are the best for maintaining cognitive fitness, but everyone seems to agree that the axiom "use it or lose it" applies, especially as we get older. The geneses for this book, then, are the beliefs that we should exercise our brains to keep them healthy and that working on puzzles is a great way to get that mental exercise.

So, this book offers you a bountiful menu of seven types of puzzles with which to get your brain exercise, including the perennial favorites crossword and Sudoku, two other number logic puzzles (Calcudoku and Futoshiki), narrative logic puzzles, cryptograms, and word search puzzles. Calcudoku is a twin brother to the KenKen that you might have tried before; Futoshiki is like a Calcudoku, except that the puzzle uses a few seeded numbers and strategically placed inequality signs (>) to show in what order the numbers should appear in the completed grid.

The book's variety of puzzles ensures that you will give a number of your mental "muscles" a good workout. This is important because experts believe you maximize your brain exercise benefits by exercising as many different brain functions as possible. With seven types of puzzles, this book could enable you to focus on a different type of puzzle each day of the week if you choose to tackle the puzzles that way.

Each of the puzzle types is introduced in a preliminary chapter entitled "Getting Started," which provides a sample puzzle along with a brief discussion of my take on which mental skills are used and strengthened by working that type of puzzle, a summary explanation of how the puzzle works, and some tips on how to get started in solving it.

The puzzles are presented in three groups—easier, medium, and more challenging. This gradation of difficulty will give you a chance to develop your puzzling skills before you tackle the tougher puzzles that stretch your mental "muscles" the most. And, it allows you to push your limits as you work your way through the book, which facilitates the strengthening of your brain's cognitive functions. Just in case, the solutions to all the puzzles (along with answers to several trivia questions that pop up throughout the book) are provided in a final chapter (see page 123).

Finally, the puzzles have been crafted to make them accessible to people who aren't already experts at a particular type of puzzle and, more importantly, to ensure they are fun to work on as well as challenging. My hope is that you will make it through all the puzzles in the book and that, when you are finished, you will be ready to come back for more.

CHAPTER 1
GETTING STARTED

BRAIN HEALTH EXERCISE: long-term memory, attention to detail, logic

Crosswords really test your long-term memory, or recall, of all the words you have acquired over your lifetime and stored away in your brain. However, a crossword is not just a vocabulary test. Far from it. Crosswords challenge you in other ways. They require your attention to detail and encourage you to flex your reasoning "muscles," as when a clue doesn't just define the word that is the entry but indirectly suggests the answer. You will find that, in each of this book's crosswords, close to half the clues are of this indirect variety.

HOW TO SOLVE: It is not complicated—just fill in every Across and Down entry on the puzzle grid, based on the information provided in the set of clues.

TIPS FOR SOLVING

» Rather than try to solve each of the clues in the order they appear in the clue list, you can make better progress by scanning the clues to find answers you can fill in right away. These entries will give you footholds to build clusters of crossing words. To make additional footholds, you can (tentatively) fill in word fragments like an -s at the end of an entry that the clue indicates is a plural noun or an -ed at the end of an entry that the clue indicates is a past-tense verb.

» You should look for obvious and not-so-obvious directional hints contained in the clues. If an entry is an abbreviation, the clue might signal that by including an abbreviation. Or, if the clue reads something like "Arles article," you can deduce that, since Arles is in France, the clue is asking you to name the French word for the article "a"—UNE.

» Also, be on the lookout for an occasional clue ending in a question mark. That tells you that the constructor is giving an unusual pun meaning to the answer that is not at all obvious. Further, the answer might be related to another answer in the puzzle that explains the not-obvious relationship between the clue and its answer. In short, be prepared to think outside the box when you spot a question mark.

» Finally, a note about obscure entries—words you are unlikely to have encountered before. Sometimes, the constructor needs to use such a word to make the rest of the words in the puzzle all fit together nicely. I've kept these words to a tiny handful in this book, and the way to deal with any word you are stumped on is to work around it by solving the entries that cross with it.

ACROSS

1. Cuts calories
6. Out of harm's way
10. Washer cycle
14. Boredom
15. Blueprint
16. Assistant
17. Gizmo
20. Places for experiments
21. The "I" in TGIF
22. Estimator's phrase
23. "Is that ___?"
24. Gridiron gains: Abbr.
25. Originator
28. Squinted
30. "___ bien!"
31. Anger
32. "Relax, private!"
34. Nose-in-the-air type
35. Gizmo
38. Ogles
40. Sports venues
41. CD follower
42. Derbies and bowlers
44. Comes up
48. Highest ranking
50. Roker and Pacino
51. Not well
52. Irish word for Ireland
53. AFL's partner: Init.
54. ___-European languages
55. Animated crime-fighter whose last name is roughly equivalent to "Gizmo"
59. Mechanistic learning method
60. ___ and hearty
61. Edible part of a fruit
62. An "A" in NCAA: Abbr.
63. Memorable periods
64. Exams

DOWN

1. Turkey's wattle, e.g.
2. Take a breath
3. Empower
4. Sounds of reproof
5. [not my error]
6. Tiffs
7. "___ for the poor"
8. Air traffic regulatory agency: Init.
9. Concert bonus
10. Latin dance
11. Flying (a plane)
12. First name in tyranny
13. Court divider
18. Concealed
19. Bellicose deity
24. Legendary Himalayan creature
25. ___ brûlée (dessert)
26. Guadalajara gold
27. Confederate soldier, for short
29. Stadium cheers
30. Autocrats of old
33. Quartz variety
34. Emphatic assent in Acapulco
35. Violent storms
36. Like clocks with hands
37. Glass containers
38. Triage sites, briefly
39. "___ rang?"
42. Epitaph starter
43. Don _____ (movie star in the 1930s and 1940s and then again in the 1980s)
45. Scorches
46. Firstborn
47. Tree-dwelling mammals
49. Turn red, say
50. Buenos _____, Arg.
53. Pepsi, for one
54. Inactive
55. George Gershwin's brother
56. Figures: Abbr.
57. Besmirch
58. Astern

№1 GIZMOS

1 D	2 I	3 E	4 T	5 S		6 S	7 A	8 F	9 E		10 S	11 P	12 I	13 N
14 E	N	N	U	I		15 P	L	A	N		16 A	I	D	E
17 W	H	A	T	C	18 H	A	M	A	C	19 A	L	L	I	T
20 L	A	B	S		21 I	T	S		22 O	R	S	O		
23 A	L	L		24 Y	D	S		25 C	R	E	A	T	26 O	27 R
28 P	E	E	R	E	29 D		30 T	R	E	S		31 I	R	E
			32 A	T	E	33 A	S	E			34 S	N	O	B
		35 T	H	I	N	G	A	M	36 A	37 J	I	G		
38 E	39 Y	E	S		40 A	R	E	N	A	S				
41 R	O	M		42 H	43 A	T	S		44 A	R	I	45 S	46 E	47 S
48 S	U	P	49 R	E	M	E		50 A	L	S		51 I	L	L
		52 E	I	R	E		53 C	I	D		54 I	N	D	O
55 I	56 N	S	P	E	C	57 T	O	R	G	58 A	D	G	E	T
59 R	O	T	E		60 H	A	L	E		61 F	L	E	S	H
62 A	S	S	N		63 E	R	A	S		64 T	E	S	T	S

THINK ABOUT IT

All the major organizations that study brain health agree that to maintain a healthy brain you must be intellectually engaged and active.

BRAIN HEALTH EXERCISE: attention to detail, spatial abilities, short-term memory

Word searches might be considered the least complex of the puzzles in this book, but they still offer tons of brain exercise. They require great attention to detail and intense focus. I can't tell you how many times I have searched in vain for a word embedded in the word search grid when it was sitting there staring me in the face if I had only focused hard enough. Also, since the puzzles in this book are embedded in the grid every which way—backward, vertically, upside down, and diagonally, as well as horizontally reading left to right—you will be required to engage your brain's spatial functions and use your short-term working memory to recognize those harder-to-envision embedded words. Your short-term memory is also tested as you keep the word you are searching for at the front of your mind while you scan the grid for it.

HOW TO SOLVE: Scan the puzzle grid to find all the words in the key words list below the grid, and mark the words as you find them by circling or striking through them.

TIPS FOR SOLVING

» Keep in mind that, since key words can be embedded in the grid diagonally, backward, and upside down, any given letter in the grid might be part of a key word running in any of eight different directions. Game on!

» I am not aware of any set method for visually scanning the entirety of the grid looking for key words. Some like to start out by looking for key words with easy-to-spot letters in them, like O, Q, and I (or whatever other letter jumps out at you visually). Others might prefer to start scanning the grid by looking for double letters, such as the TT in LETTER.

» Another way to customize your search is to pick several key words starting with the same letter and scan the grid for all of them at the same time. It's an efficient use of your scanning time and effort, but it does require you to push the limits of your short-term memory.

№ 1 TAKE ME OUT TO THE BALLGAME

```
C I B O N D R A O B E R O C S
S T N A F L Y B A L L T G P K
R H U F T N A F O U L L I N E
E W O O I S S A X I K T N Y N
H S E M E E B G N I C N U F U
C E D B E K L N O H A P R Q R
A G A N L P I D E D R U A T E
E L L A A N L R B S T P O U M
L R B O G T S A T M G O Q O O
B O H S V M S E T S N P H G H
T R N R O E A D L E I F T U O
N R E U H L S S I G N S Q D Y
U E N I T B A T T E R S B O X
B D T U M P I R E B A S E S Y
S T U N A E P Q N S W I N G T
```

BALK	DUGOUT	INNINGS	STEAL
BASEBALL	ERROR	OUTFIELD	STRIKE OUT
BASE HIT	FLY BALL	PEANUTS	SWING
BASES	FOUL LINE	PITCHER'S MOUND	TURF
BATS	GLOVES	POP-UP	UMPIRE
BATTER'S BOX	HOME PLATE	RUN	WARNING TRACK
BEER	HOME RUN	SCOREBOARD	
BLEACHERS	HOT DOGS	SIGNS	
BUNT	INFIELD	STANDS	

BRAIN HEALTH EXERCISE: logic, long-term memory, pattern recognition

The code used in a cryptogram (which is a straightforward substitution of one letter for another) can only be broken by the application of logic, combined with use of your long-term memory of how English words and sentences are structured. Decoding also involves creative thinking/inductive logic and the use of pattern recognition (looking for repeated use of certain letter combinations) as you develop hypotheses as to what various encoded groups of letters might mean.

HOW TO SOLVE: Each cryptogram consists of an encoded quotation of something said by a well-known person and that person's name. To help you get started, we offer you hints that decode from one to three letters used in the cryptogram, but you don't have to use the hints if you don't want to.

TIPS FOR SOLVING

» You should look for clues given by the structure of the words in the cryptogram. For example, a one-letter word is an A or I 99.9 percent of the time, and a letter following an apostrophe most likely is an S or T.

» I am always on the lookout for a three-letter word that is positioned like it might be "THE" and testing out those letters in other parts of the cryptogram.

» Be sure to check to see if a word is repeated in the puzzle, as that commonly happens.

» Don't forget the title of the puzzle, especially if you are halfway or further along in decoding the letters. The title might give you a good hint as you try to visualize, even with a lot of gaps in the wording, what the overall text of the quotation is driving at.

№1 LET'S BE PRACTICAL

FKQNK LHQBMQBY QB MKO BHMQJBHI YHIIOVD

_____

FJEIT Q GHCO QR MKOVO FHG H RQVO? MKO JBO

_____

BOHVOGM MKO TJJV JR NJEVGO.

_____

—YOJVYO POVBHVT GKHF

_____

HINTS (SEE PAGE 124): 11, 17, 30

BRAIN HEALTH EXERCISE: deductive logic, attention to detail, short-term memory

Solving a Sudoku is an exercise in deductive logic, determining with certainty, in each case, that a cell in the grid can contain one and only one out of the nine possible digits. It also involves great attention to detail and use of your short-term memory as you look for pathways to confirming a number's place in a cell, which might involve two or more steps in the process.

HOW TO SOLVE: The challenge of a Sudoku is to fill each empty cell in the grid with a number 1 through 9, so that each row across, each column down, and each 3x3 cage contains all the numbers 1 through 9 with no repeats.

TIPS FOR SOLVING

» It is usually a good idea to start by working through each numeral, from 1 through 9, to see if the grid already contains enough iterations of a certain number that you can deduce where one or more of the other iterations must appear.

» Then, I prefer to use the "rule of 5," under which I look for a row, column, or cage already filled with five or more of the numbers 1 through 9 and then see if I can deduce where one or more the remaining four or fewer numbers must go based on the layout of filled cells at that time. This exercise stands a reasonable chance of yielding a determination as to the location of at least one, but possibly more, of the remaining numbers.

» Once that exercise is completed, then it is a matter of analyzing the information now on the grid (including the info you have added) to look for further solutions based on pure logic.

SUDOKU №1

4	5		7		6		2	
	8		3	5	2		4	
		6						
9	4	2						
			1		9			
						9	7	5
						7		
	1		8	4	3		5	
	9		2		7		1	4

BRAIN HEALTH EXERCISE: logic, short-term memory

Solving a Calcudoku requires the use of deductive logic, determining with certainty in what order the numbers in a row or column must appear. The grid "cages" and inserts give you a starting point from which, using inductive logic, you can develop hypotheses as to what numbers could fit into the cage. Then, relying on your short-term memory, you try out your hypotheses in your head. If one doesn't work, you go on to try other combinations until you find the right one.

HOW TO SOLVE: Calcudoku is a number logic puzzle like Sudoku but differs in that its puzzle grid contains cages that vary in size and each cage has inserted in the upper left corner a number with a arithmetic symbol indicating addition, subtraction, multiplication, or division (the symbol for which in this book is :, not ÷). That insert tells you that, when you apply the arithmetic function to the numbers you propose to insert in the cage, they must result in the insert number. Single-cell cages simply designate the number that is intended to go in the cell.

TIPS FOR SOLVING

» Start by filling in the "slam dunk" single-cell cages right away and then pencil in lightly (because you don't know what order they will appear in the grid) numbers in cages that can contain only those numbers. For example, a two-cell cage with an insert reading "15x" can only contain 3 and 5 in some order.

» Next, look for any information you have in a crossing row or column that can confirm where, in the 15x example, the 3 and 5 belong within the cage.

» Then, it is a matter of winkling out every number placement that the limited information in the grid will support and you can spot.

» Don't forget that you can always put your review of the cages aside and apply the most basic Sudoku technique of scanning each row and column of the grid that has some filled-in numbers to see if some obvious placement of another number in an empty cell is in order.

CALCUDOKU №1

FUTOSHIKI

BRAIN HEALTH EXERCISE: deductive logic, spatial abilities, short-term memory

Solving a Futoshiki requires application of deductive logic, along with spatial reasoning as you visually follow inequality signs as they connect cells in different columns and rows of the grid. As the puzzles increase in difficulty, they require you to lean heavily on your short-term memory as you try to picture in your mind what the consequences might be of opting for a choice of number placements.

HOW TO SOLVE: A Futoshiki, like Sudoku and Calcudoku, is a number logic puzzle. What distinguishes it is that it doesn't use "cages" within the grid to convey information about missing numbers—instead, it uses a few seeded numbers and strategically placed inequality signs (>) to show in what order the numbers should appear in the completed grid. For example, 3 followed by a > to the right of it on the grid means that the number to the right of it can only be a 2 or a 1.

TIPS FOR SOLVING

» Focus on extended series of connected inequality signs. If you can peg the number in a cell in that sequence, you gain a lot of information on what other numbers in the sequence might be.

» Be on the alert that a 1 can never be larger than another number and that if, for example, the grid measures 6x6, a 6 can never be smaller than another number.

» As with Calcudoku, don't forget that you can put your review of the inequality signs aside and apply the most basic Sudoku technique of scanning each row and column of the grid that has some filled-in numbers to see if some obvious placement of another number in an empty cell is in order.

FUTOSHIKI №1

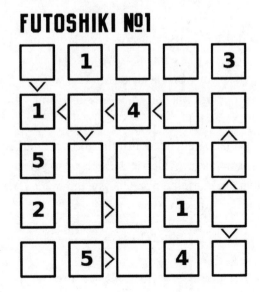

LOGIC PUZZLES

BRAIN HEALTH EXERCISE: deductive logic, spatial reasoning, attention to detail

Narrative logic puzzles for the most part involve deductive logic (if a car color can't be green, blue, or red, it must be the only option left—white). Also, the logic puzzle grid is a powerful tool to enable you to solve the puzzle when used to the full extent of its potential. But, to take advantage of that potential, you must be able to read what the data points on the grid created by the negative check marks and positive stars tell you about other empty boxes in the grid. That really puts a premium on spatial reasoning. Scrupulous attention to detail, however, is equally critical to successfully filling out a logic puzzle grid. Innumerable times, I have found that I missed one small detail in a clue that, once it is brought into play, creates a domino effect leading to elimination of a number of related options.

HOW TO SOLVE: Narrative logic puzzles ask you to tie together various items in several categories based on statements about the items provided as clues. Essential to working a logic puzzle is the grid, which converts the language-based information you deduce from clues into abstract spatial concepts. You use it by putting checks or Xs in boxes that you know are false ("Jim's car is not blue") and stars in the boxes you know are true ("Joe's car is red"). Why do that? You will see, as you work a logic puzzle, that this conversion process enables you to use the information you have extracted from the clues to deduce conclusions about options the clues don't address. So, as you work your way through the clues, check off the grid boxes for various possibilities as they are eliminated.

TIPS FOR SOLVING

> » As the grid develops a lot of negative check marks and some positive stars, you should be able, by applying spatial reasoning, to reach deductive conclusions that allow you to place positive stars next to an item without there having been a positive statement about the item in the list of clues, or even any statement directly touching on the item.

> » Focus, focus, focus! Did you read the clues correctly and capture all the ramifications of a clue on the grid? Did you place the negative check mark in the correct box in the grid? (If you mess up, the error won't likely be obvious, and only after working a lot further in your analysis of clues will you come to a dead end, which means you will have to start over from scratch.)

> » Keep in mind that information encoded into the grid later in the analysis can reshape the significance of information provided in early clues, so you should go back over the clues again once you've completed an analysis and marked up the grid initially to see what other conclusions you can reach.

№1 NEW KITTENS IN THE NEIGHBORHOOD

Four kittens from a litter born out in the country have found their way to the city and into the homes of four families that live close to one another. Each of the families has children who got to name the new arrivals. As the kittens get acclimated to their new surroundings, see if you can figure out each kitten's new name, what color they are, and the family they are becoming part of.

1. Besides Fluffy (who is not the kitten being adopted by the Janney family), there is the gray kitten and the kitten that will reside with the Johnsons.

2. Neither Rascal nor the Janneys' kitten is a calico.

3. Mr. Whiskers is not joining the Johns household.

4. The Jeffries' kitten isn't being named Rascal; the Johnsons' kitten isn't being named Twinkie.

5. The gray kitten has been given the name of Mr. Whiskers but will not be joining the Janney family.

6. Twinkie is not black or calico.

		black	calico	gray	gray & white	Janney	Jeffries	Johns	Johnson
Kitten	Fluffy								
	Rascal								
	Mr. Whiskers								
	Twinkie								
Family	Janney								
	Jeffries								
	Johns								
	Johnson								

CHAPTER 2
PUZZLES ON THE EASIER SIDE

CROSSWORD

ACROSS

1. Passed with flying colors
5. English race place
10. _____ Lee baked goods
14. U2 singer
15. "Odyssey" enchantress
16. Pare
17. Situation of financial comfort
19. Bank take-back, for short
20. Early anesthetics
21. Cultural Revolution leader
22. Unique person, slangily
23. Genetic initials
24. 1967 Beatles hit
26. Person performing some oral hygiene
29. Gal in a song
30. Lac contents
31. Some offspring
34. Tart fruit
38. Moderate, avoiding extremes
42. Befuddled
43. Exercise target
44. Curator's degree: Init.
45. Corker
47. Like open convertibles or some beaches
50. Hard hit baseball
55. Aachen article
56. Norse war god
57. Stop-dime link
58. In fine _____ (fit)
61. Cattail, e.g.
62. Written documentation
64. Minnow kin
65. Foe
66. Cupid, to the Greeks
67. Downhill coaster
68. Take to court again
69. "Auld Lang _____"

DOWN

1. Busy as _____
2. Jacket
3. Envelops completely
4. Senior members of a group
5. *Hamlet* has five
6. Knight's title
7. Cookie filling
8. Watery expanse
9. Mountains in Wyoming
10. Baby transport
11. *Gladiator* setting
12. Mature
13. Love, in Livorno
18. Mmes., in Madrid
24. Verification
25. Harvard rival
26. Disaster relief agcy.: Init.
27. Café lightener
28. 180° from WNW
32. Ravens' and Eagles' org.: Init.
33. Express definitely
35. Brief
36. Lummoxes
37. Secret-keeping contracts, for short
39. Hinged (on)
40. Put down
41. Cable channel
46. Suitable, appropriate
48. Actress Amanda _____
49. British capacity measures
50. Some British noblemen
51. Model
52. Family girl
53. Silly
54. Has an e-cig
58. Popular boot brand
59. Big cat
60. Besides
63. Ostrich cousin

№2 HIGHWAYS AND BYWAYS

1 A	2	3	4		5	6	7	8	9		10	11	12	13
14 B O N O					15						16			
17 E			18								19			
20 E						21				22				
		23			24			25						
26	27			28			29							
30				31		32	33		34		35	36	37	
38		39	40					41						
42				43						44				
		45		46			47		48	49				
50	51	52			53	54			55					
56				57			58				59	60		
61				62		63								
64				65					66					
67				68					69					

DID YOU KNOW?

Edgar Allan Poe loved puzzles and had a thing about cryptograms. As a magazine editor, he challenged readers to send him substitution ciphers (like the cryptograms in this book) to decode, and he solved all that were sent in. One of his most famous short stories, "The Gold Bug," included a cryptogram as a key plot element.

ACROSS

1. Sales agents, briefly
5. Competent
9. Couch
13. Off-ramps
15. Bridle strap
16. Clickable image
17. Infant's woe
18. "One if by _____ . . ."
19. Blowgun missile
20. Big hit song by Elvis
23. Get goose bumps
24. Legalese adverb
27. High card
28. First appearance on stage
30. Hindu queen
31. Scandinavian man's name
33. Hound, badger
34. Many a cruise stop
35. Discharged a debt
37. Run _____ (go wild)
38. How long one might stay
41. Small bite
42. Buy's opposite
46. _____ of America
47. Hearing related
49. Potpie morsel
50. Charge borrowers pay
52. Mascara targets
54. Exercise machines that combine lower- and upper-body workouts
56. Qatar's capital
58. Radial, e.g.
59. CBer's equipment
60. Opposite of "sans"
61. Sugar suffixes
62. Binge
63. Halloween purchase
64. Artist Mondrian
65. Early 2000s virus outbreak, briefly

DOWN

1. Carnegie Hall offering
2. Unusual stuff
3. Light lager
4. Sharp pain
5. Woody's son
6. Hearty greeting
7. Old World songbird
8. Rear-_____ (common type of car crash)
9. Hopscotch sites
10. Simple wind instrument
11. In favor of
12. Aardvark's morsel
14. Bawl out
21. Hot dog
22. Left-hand page
25. Gymnast's goal
26. "If only ___ listened . . ."
29. Defective
32. Kitchen receptacle for items like sage and cumin
34. African antelope
36. Last Oldsmobile model
37. Make public
38. Bird: Prefix
39. Took the gold
40. Thumbs a ride
41. Pecan or hazel, say
43. Diet supplement banned since 2004
44. More suspicious
45. Rodeo ropes
47. Birthplace of St. Francis
48. Hideouts
51. Bar, at the bar
53. Ginger cookies
55. Unwind
56. Hydroelectric project
57. Eggs: Lat.

№3 TRACES OF PRECIP

THINK ABOUT IT

How busy an organ is the human brain? So busy that the body allocates large amounts of its resources to keep it functioning. Even though the brain makes up only about 2 percent of the body's total weight, it consumes more than 20 percent of the body's energy.

ACROSS

1. Font flourish
6. Yves Saint Laurent perfume named after a narcotic
11. Extinct flightless bird
14. Madison Square Garden, e.g.
15. Fastidious
16. Coat part
17. Popular side
19. 2016 Olympics site
20. Immigrant's class: Init.
21. Coin flip call
22. "You don't _____ Superman's cape" (Croce lyric)
24. Scatters, as seeds
25. Ventilating
26. Eggs Benedict ingredient
31. Mock
32. Be _____ in the ointment (cause a minor problem)
33. Gorilla
36. Stuck in _____ (bogged down)
37. Sis's sib
38. Lost traction
39. May honoree
40. Feathery scarves
42. Making cow sounds
44. Cured meat delicacy
47. Helix
49. Division word
50. Laser printer powder
51. Desert flora
53. Carrier to Tokyo: Init.
56. Rage
57. Cousins of sorbets
60. ____ Liaisons Dangereuses
61. Katmandu's land
62. Clutch
63. Sheeran, Helms, and Asner
64. High renown
65. SNL staples

DOWN

1. Ump's call
2. Goofs up
3. Country dance
4. B & B
5. Trivial bit of information
6. Aloof
7. "Knit one, _____ two"
8. Egyptian goddess
9. Avail oneself of
10. Bewilder utterly
11. Notes scribbled alongside the text
12. Betelgeuse's constellation
13. In the midst of
18. Hole for an anchor cable
23. Psychic ____ Geller
24. Narrow opening
25. Half of a 1955 merger of unions: Init.
26. Dutch cheese
27. Adopted son of Claudius
28. Characteristic of being irritable and crabby
29. Swamp
30. Roswell sighting: Init.
34. Unwelcome engine sound
35. Rim
37. ____-relief
38. Mediocre
40. Making a loud, harsh sound
41. Black gold
42. Kind of ray
43. Excursions
45. Mine find
46. Mount Etna's island
47. Steps over a fence
48. Read very carefully (with "over")
51. Mafia bigwig
52. Banned apple spray
53. Smoothie berry
54. Hatchling's home
55. Nile reptiles
58. ____ Aviv, Israel
59. Irritate

№ 4 FOOD WITH AN INTERNATIONAL FLAIR

1	2	3	4	5		6	7	8	9	10		11	12	13
14						15						16		
17				18								19		
20				21						22	23			
			24						25					
26	27	28					29	30						
31						32					33	34	35	
36					37				38					
39				40	41				42	43				
		44	45				46							
47	48						49							
50					51	52					53	54	55	
56				57	58					59				
60				61					62					
63				64					65					

1950S TRIVIA CHALLENGE

Republican Dwight Eisenhower was elected president twice in the 1950s. Who was his Democratic opponent in both elections?

Who sold more cars in the 1950s, Chevy or Ford?

ACROSS

1. 11,000-foot Italian peak
5. Internet automatons
9. D-Day beach
14. Pad _____ (noodle dish)
15. D-Day beach
16. Office records
17. Important indicator to a palm reader
19. Coquette
20. ___ de Triomphe
21. Chicago trains
22. Summer thirst quencher
24. Neighbor of Tibet
26. Single-handedly
27. Diner menu item
33. Scourge
36. "___ 'em!" (command to a dog)
37. English exam finale, often
38. Obamacare initials
39. Stock up on again
42. Sass
43. *Ted* _____
45. Helpful connections
46. French door part
47. NL West team
51. Dean Martin's "That's _____"
52. Modern surgical tool
56. Turn down
59. Quiche, e.g.
61. Caroler's syllable
62. "Skyfall" singer
63. Preliminary activity
66. Challenges
67. Bone-dry
68. Not windward
69. Sting
70. Tibetan bovines
71. Many wines

DOWN

1. Actor Hawke
2. Not 12-Down
3. Civil rights org.: Init.
4. Melody
5. Wall Street optimist
6. Elevator inventor
7. Yellowish-brown
8. Aussie lassie
9. Wrongdoer
10. Fungal growths
11. Landed
12. Not 2-Down
13. *The Thin Man* canine
18. Blab
23. Bamboozle
25. Highest card in every suit
26. Attribute
28. Finish, with "up"
29. Life story, briefly
30. Ibiza, por ejemplo
31. Genesis son
32. Hoopla
33. _____ eagle
34. Trendy berry
35. Canaveral org.: Init.
39. Most spacious
40. Genetic initials
41. Bailout key
44. More petite
46. Pro bono TV ad: Init.
48. Oui's opposite
49. Like formal clothing
50. *Twittering Machine* artist
53. Fur wrap
54. Made a mistake
55. Tidies the lawn
56. June honorees
57. Gouda alternative
58. Michael _____ of *Arrested Development*
59. Place for picnicking
60. Bad day for Caesar
64. ___ shooter
65. Children's card game

№5 SUITS

1	2	3	4		5	6	7	8		9	10	11	12	13
14					15					16				
17			18						19					
20				21			22	23						
24			25			26								
			27		28	29						30	31	32
33	34	35			36				37					
38			39				40	41			42			
43			44			45				46				
47				48	49				50					
			51						52		53	54	55	
56	57	58					59	60			61			
62					63	64				65				
66					67					68				
69					70					71				

DID YOU KNOW?

Experts tell us that the 12 most-commonly used letters in the English language (in their order of appearance) are E T A O I N S R H L D C and that these letters appear in about 80 percent of all English words.

ACROSS

1. "Assuming that's true . . ."
5. Fortune teller
9. Cézanne contemporary
14. Not slack
15. Toy that does tricks
16. Blow one's top
17. Bronzed, in a way
19. Tilts, as a ship
20. Takes over
21. Colossal
23. Apple virtual assistant
24. Human spirit
25. Rehab symptoms: Init.
28. WWI battle site
31. Floor plan
33. Atmosphere: Prefix
36. Cascades peak
38. Leave in, as text
40. Mutual of _____
41. Encounter
42. 1960s sitcom about a family headed by a dad who looks like Frankenstein's monster and a mom who's a vampire
45. "Understand?"
46. Bar request
47. Alleviated
49. ____ longa, vita brevis
50. Puppy sounds
52. Pot
55. Analogy phrase
56. Orders of business
59. Appears
62. Planters offering . . . and a hint regarding this puzzle's circled letters
64. Pond buildup
65. Genesis garden
66. Rapper turned actor
67. Grabs (onto)
68. Agree (with)
69. Homilies: Abbr.

DOWN

1. "_____ girl!"
2. Pastoral deities
3. Certain Muslim
4. Frolicking aquatic animals
5. Word in song sung very early on January 1
6. Almost forever
7. Hurricane's center
8. Cowboy competition
9. Samson's temptress
10. Singer Clapton
11. Gloomy guy
12. Fitting
13. Avenue crossers: Abbr.
18. Accepted truth
22. Small, dense stars
24. Upper houses
25. Medicinal amounts
26. Student getting one-on-one help
27. Express
29. Like a romantic evening, maybe
30. Autumn bloomers
32. Sweet potato
33. Stars: Lat.
34. Anesthetic that's no longer used
35. Atoll features
37. Mother of Helios
39. "You're oversharing!": Init.
43. James Joyce book
44. Did some tailoring
48. Menace of comics
51. Fleshy fruits such as apples and pears
53. Draw forth
54. Anagram for TRADE
55. Muslim leader
56. Fired
57. Heredity carrier
58. Concordes: Init.
59. Droop
60. Building addition
61. Claudius's "I"
63. A mean Amin

№6 A BIT OF WORDPLAY

1	2	3	4		5	6	7	8		9	10	11	12	13
14					15					16				
17				18						19				
20							21	22						
	23					24					25	26	27	
			28		29	30			31		32			
33	34	35		36			37							
38			39		40					41				
42			43						44		45			
46					47				48					
49				50		51			52		53	54		
		55					56	57					58	
59	60	61			62	63								
64					65					66				
67					68					69				

THINK ABOUT IT

Mentally stimulating activities build what is called the "cognitive reserve," which is an ability of the brain, developed through experience, to improvise in executing some mental functions. This ability, in turn, can help people compensate for age-related brain changes and health conditions that affect the brain.

ACROSS

1. Accumulate
6. Drum kit cymbals
11. Flat-panel screen type: Init.
14. Roadside resting place
15. *La Bohème*, e.g.
16. Yellowfin tuna
17. Wavelength just beyond the purplish end of the visible spectrum
19. Bedevil
20. Nogales nap
21. Was absent from
23. Junior naval officer: Abbr.
24. Football complement
27. Time _____ half
29. _____ good example
31. Prep for publication
32. Country just south of Egypt
33. *Tootsie* Oscar winner
35. Diner
36. Author of *The Color Purple*
38. *Get Shorty* novelist Leonard
40. Obliterate
41. Christopher of *Superman*
42. _____ a Manger fast-food chain
43. Bucks' mates
47. Assign stars to
48. Paleontologist's find
50. Fuel additive: Init.
51. State of being under someone's control
53. Like a wine bouquet that has more of a woody note
55. Your of yore
56. Fruit that is dark purple when ripe
59. Notes before mis
60. Drive away
61. Offer one's two cents
62. Paintings, e.g.
63. Test, as ore
64. Stair part

DOWN

1. Brings a smile to
2. One of the Quad Cities
3. Swear (to)
4. Sunday talks: Abbr.
5. List of candidates
6. ___ polloi
7. Nasdaq debut: Init.
8. Cyclist's protection
9. "The results _____!"
10. Displays on one's skin, briefly
11. Aromatic shrub with purple flowers
12. Popular cheese
13. NJ fort
18. Ornamental drape
22. Panfried
25. Border
26. Nielsen count
28. Beginning for how, one, or where
30. Finished
32. Nordstrom rival
34. Million or concession ending
35. Jubilance
36. Purple gemstone
37. Mars, to the Greeks
38. It is said to be human to do this
39. Shoe material
42. Coral colony members
44. Egyptian god of the underworld
45. Forever, poetically
46. More nimble
48. Arctic ice sheets
49. Part of a repair bill
52. Start of a magician's cry
54. French military cap
55. "La la" preceder
57. Last word of "America, the Beautiful"
58. English cathedral city

№7 THE PURPLE GANG

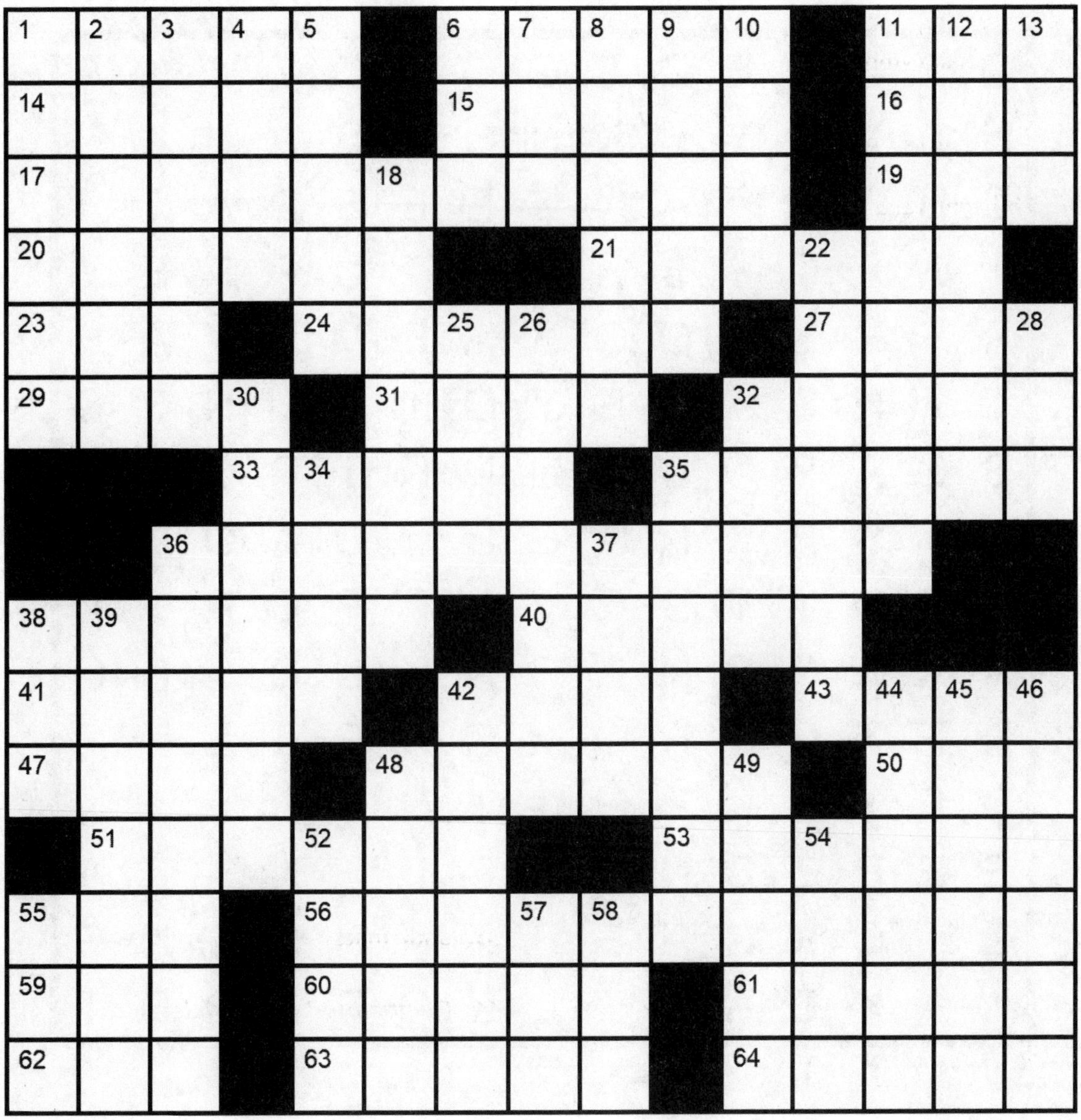

1960S TRIVIA CHALLENGE

Who was the star and eponym of a popular 1960s TV sitcom set in the fictional town of Mayberry, North Carolina?

What is the name of the NASA mission that, in 1969, put humans on the moon for the first time?

№2 AFRICAN ANIMALS

```
Q E L L E Z A G W R Q T W K A
H L Y E Y E K N O M S A U L N
C H I M P A N Z E E S D A I E
I W P O S L E M E T U P K E Y
R F H S N O O B A B M A Y A H
T W K S A Q E Y O I A M R L C
S G A P O D E N N R T B G R N
O I S R L R A E D Q O A O D I
O R S I T B E V L C P C R I L
A A W N O H A C N E O Q I K O
R F X G Q R O M O D P J L D G
B F Y B K P H G I N P H L I N
E E R O D N A L E F I N A K A
Z I O K C H E E T A H H S N P
L A K C A J T L E O P A R D T
```

AARDVARK	DIK-DIK	IMPALA	PANGOLIN
ASP	ELAND	JACKAL	RHINOCEROS
BABOON	ELEPHANT	KUDU	SPRINGBOK
BONABO	GAZELLE	LEOPARD	WARTHOG
CHEETAH	GIRAFFE	LION	WILDEBEEST
CHIMPANZEE	GORILLA	MONKEY	ZEBRA
COBRA	HIPPOPOTAMUS	ORYX	
CROCODILE	HYENA	OSTRICH	

№3 APPLES

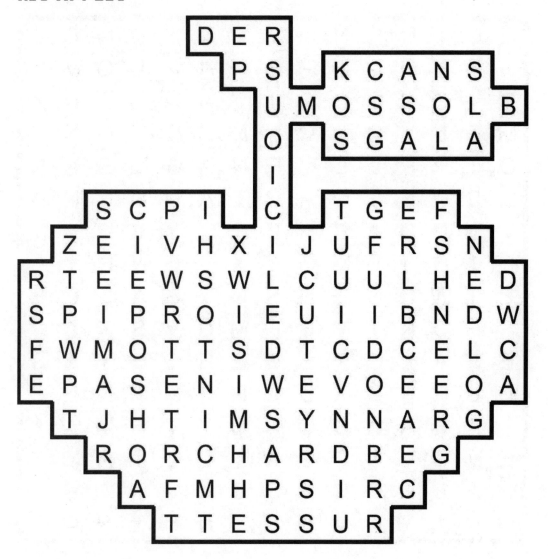

```
          D E R
          P S     K C A N S
          U   M O S S O L B
          O   S G A L A
          I
S C P I    C     T G E F
Z E I V H X I J U F R S N
R T E E W S W L C U U L H E D
S P I P R O I E U I I B N D W
F W M O T T S D T C D C E L C
E P A S E N I W E V O E E O A
T J H T I M S Y N N A R G
R O R C H A R D B E G
A F M H P S I R C
T T E S S U R
```

BLOSSOM	GALA	ORCHARD	SWEET
CIDER	GOLDEN	PIE	TART
CORE	GRANNY SMITH	PIPS	TREE
CRISP	GREEN	RED	WINESAP
DELICIOUS	JUICE	RUSSET	
FRUIT	MCINTOSH	SLICES	
FUJI	MOTTS	SNACK	

```
E  C  I  U  K  N  O  S  I  N  E  D  Q  C  D
N  K  F  H  P  O  M  O  N  A  R  L  O  M  E
B  I  O  N  O  S  D  I  V  A  D  L  F  R  X
M  E  L  Y  Q  L  C  N  N  C  G  S  O  K  H
Q  I  R  R  L  L  Y  R  N  A  W  M  E  A  N
J  S  D  E  E  O  A  C  T  A  D  N  R  N  A
Y  M  P  D  A  B  H  E  R  I  Y  V  D  A  M
E  I  D  J  L  M  O  T  K  O  E  N  H  Y  L
L  T  W  Q  N  E  H  S  N  Y  S  A  B  E  E
S  H  U  K  I  M  B  E  M  U  V  S  R  L  P
E  F  A  L  O  T  S  U  R  E  O  E  Y  S  S
L  U  P  R  D  X  D  C  R  S  M  M  N  E  B
L  R  E  A  W  D  O  F  C  Y  T  B  M  W  Z
E  M  D  V  O  L  O  W  I  L  L  I  A  M  S
W  A  L  N  B  R  A  S  S  A  V  X  W  R  V
D  N  I  Y  D  M  L  L  E  N  N  I  R  G  D
```

AMHERST	DAVIDSON	KENYON	ST. OLAF
BARD	DENISON	MIDDLEBURY	SWARTHMORE
BARNARD	DEPAUW	MOUNT HOLYOKE	VASSAR
BEREA	FURMAN	OBERLIN	WELLESLEY
BOWDOIN	GRINNELL	POMONA	WESLEYAN
BRYN MAWR	HARVEY MUDD	SKIDMORE	WILLIAMS
COLBY	HAVERFORD	SMITH	
COLGATE	HOLY CROSS	SPELMAN	

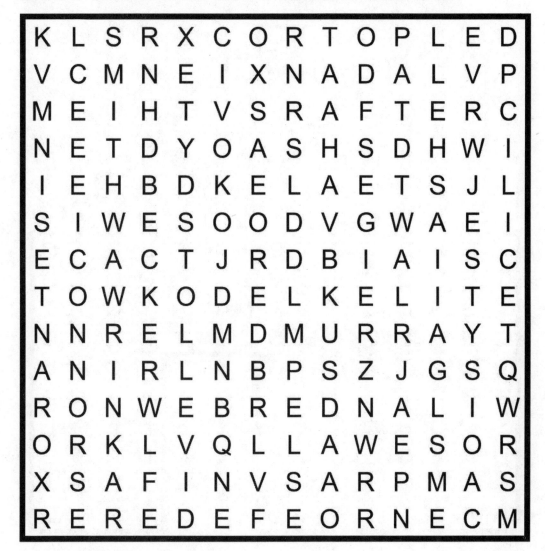

```
K L S R X C O R T O P L E D
V C M N E I X N A D A L V P
M E I H T V S R A F T E R C
N E T D Y O A S H S D H W I
I E H B D K E L A E T S J L
S I W E S O O D V G W A E I
E C A C T J R D B I A I S C
T O W K O D E L K E L I T E
N N R E L M D M U R R A Y T
A N I R L N B P S Z J G S Q
R O N W E B R E D N A L I W
O R K L V Q L L A W E S O R
X S A F I N V S A R P M A S
R E R E D E F E O R N E C M
```

AGASSI, andre
ASHE, arthur
BECKER, boris
CILIC, marin
CONNORS, jimmy
DEL POTRO, juan
DJOKOVIC, novak
EDBERG, stefan

FEDERER, roger
HEWITT, lleyton
LAVER, rod
LENDL, ivan
MCENROE, john
MEDVEDEV, daniil
MURRAY, andy
NADAL, rafael

NASTASE, ilie
NEWCOMBE, john
ORANTES, manuel
RAFTER, patrick
RODDICK, andy
ROSEWALL, ken
SAFIN, marat
SAMPRAS, pete

SMITH, stan
STOLLE, fred
THIEM, dominic
VILAS, guillermo
WAWRINKA, stan
WILANDER, mats

№6 WHERE WE LIVE

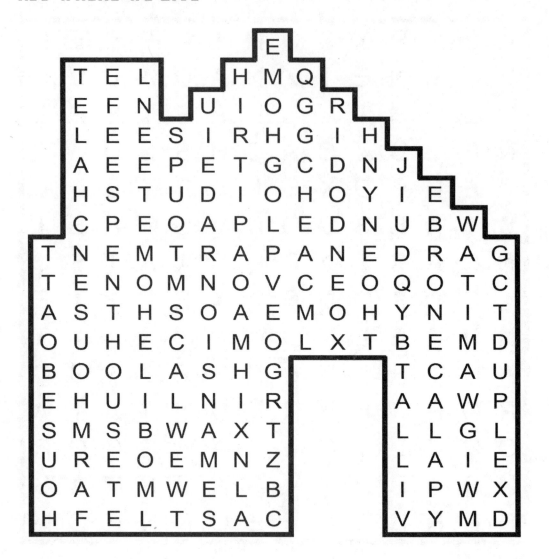

CABIN	HIGH-RISE	TENT
CASTLE	HOUSEBOAT	TEPEE
CHALET	IGLOO	TINY HOME
CONDO	LOG HOME	TOWNHOME
CO-OP	MANSION	VILLA
COTTAGE	MOBILE HOME	WIGWAM
DUPLEX	PALACE	YURT
FARMHOUSE	PENTHOUSE	
GARDEN APARTMENT	STUDIO	

```
E  Z  W  K  U  Z  O  H  A  A  X  N  E  S
Z  U  N  A  K  C  O  N  K  M  O  L  H  S
V  U  E  B  Q  F  F  L  U  N  A  V  C  E
G  H  O  U  L  T  O  O  E  W  S  L  K  R
C  A  Y  A  Q  P  H  X  Z  U  A  E  L  T
A  R  N  T  C  R  N  A  Y  D  B  V  O  K
R  K  U  Q  A  R  U  E  I  R  I  O  H  J
B  J  R  T  C  A  N  E  X  T  E  N  A  Q
E  R  E  U  T  L  U  L  H  I  I  V  D  T
Z  U  O  D  I  M  E  A  T  Y  V  I  U  T
H  P  M  O  O  Q  H  H  S  X  O  N  G  E
G  K  Q  Z  D  S  B  W  E  N  R  D  G  A
L  S  M  E  G  T  O  D  I  U  Q  S  E  C
Y  J  L  N  N  A  P  A  J  Y  K  T  B  L
```

ADIEU	HAITI	OOMPH	VIXEN
BROOD	IONIA	POLKA	WHALE
CACTI	JAPAN	QUEUE	XENON
DOZEN	KNOCK	REVUE	YODEL
ENACT	LLAMA	SQUID	ZEBRA
FLANK	MEATY	TRESS	
GHOUL	NOVEL	U-BOAT	

№2 SORTING FOLKS OUT

PSMIM QIM UQDWXQFFN PRG PNTMD GJ TMGTFM.

_____

TMGTFM RSG QXXGETFWDS PSWHBD, QHV TMGTFM

_____

RSG XFQWE PG SQKM QXXGETFWDSMV PSWHBD.

_____

PSM JWIDP BIGLT WD FMDD XIGRVMV.

_____

—EQIC PRQWH

_____

HINTS (SEE PAGE 124): 3, 14, 24

№3 IT'S OKAY TO DREAM BIG

ZX PKG SFIJ LGZUB TFHBUJH ZC BSJ FZE, PKGE OKEV

_____

CJJQ CKB LJ UKHB; BSFB ZH OSJEJ BSJP HSKGUQ LJ.

_____

CKO WGB BSJ XKGCQFBZKCH GCQJE BSJD.

_____

—SJCEP QFIZQ BSKEJFG

_____

HINTS (SEE PAGE 124): 5, 20, 23

№4 SOME FORTITUDE NEEDED HERE

JQQ GZ XF OJMP KGKPLHF TL GXB QTMPF HOJH HPFH

_____

GXB NGXBJUP. HJWTLU NOTQYBPL TLHG J OGXFP DTHO

_____

J DOTHP NJBSPH TF GLP GZ HOPK.

_____

—PBKJ VGKVPNW

_____

HINTS (SEE PAGE 124): 6, 13, 19

№5 EVERYBODY CONTRIBUTES

WPU ACBJL VE YCGUL MJCXS, XCW CXJI QI WPU

_____

YVSPWI EPCGUE CK VWE PUBCUE, QNW MJEC QI WPU

_____

MSSBUSMWU CK WVXI HNEPUE CK UMRP PCXUEW

_____

ACBOUB.

_____

—PUJUX OUJJUB

_____

HINTS (SEE PAGE 124): 28, 31, 39

№6 A SCIENCE THAT IS INHERENTLY IFFY

FV TFJ FV GIX DFNV CT SFGIXSFGURV JXTXJ GC

_____

JXFDUGP, GIXP FJX ACG RXJGFUA; FAL FV TFJ FV GI XP

_____

FJX RXJGFUA, GIXP LC ACG JXTXJ GC JXFDUGP.

_____

—FDOXJG XUAVGXUA

_____

HINTS (SEE PAGE 124): 12, 29, 36

№7 OFFSETTING GIFTS

PTYQPCYEPKC BYM QPOVC EK UFTYCM EK

_____

IKTHVCMYEV EUVT NKJ BUYE EUVL YJV CKE; Y MVCMV

_____

KN UFTKJ EK IKCMKSV EUVT NKJ BUYE EUVL YJV.

_____

—NJYCIPM RYIKC

_____

HINTS (SEE PAGE 124): 25, 33, 38

SUDOKU №2

			9	7				
		4					2	7
	6		5				3	
	5				9		8	
6			8		7			2
	3		6				9	
	2				6		1	
3	9					5		
				5	4			

SUDOKU №3

9		5						7
			1				2	6
			8	7				1
4	9							
1	8	6				3	4	2
							9	8
7				6	8			
3	4				5			
5						2		4

SUDOKU №4

								2
	7		5	2	1			
	9		6	8			1	
		2	9			5		
4	5						8	3
		3			8	7		
	2			6	5		3	
			2	7	4		9	
1								

SUDOKU №5

				4				6
3	7							9
1	2				9	5		
4	3		7			6		
		1				3		
		8			6		4	2
		7	3				5	8
6							2	1
8				2				

SUDOKU №6

9			1				5	6
		6				3		2
2	3		6	7				
		8	3				7	
		9	7		6	8		
	7				8	2		
				8	1		9	7
8		7				5		
5	4				7			8

SUDOKU №7

	8		2		7			
		1			3			
	2	7	1	8				
	1		8			6		3
	7						4	
4		9		6			7	
			1	8	5	3		
			9			7		
			4		2		8	

CALCUDOKU

CALCUDOKU №2

10+		6+	3+
	4×		
4×		4+	
		7+	

CALCUDOKU №3

10×		5+		12×
5×		24×		
5+	1-		7+	
		3	10×	
7+		5		1

CALCUDOKU №4

2×		2-	20×	
1	4		2-	1-
9+	6+			
		6+	1-	1
2-				

CALCUDOKU №5

13+	3	3-		2
		1-	3-	5+
4×	2 :			
		5+		2-
2 :		5×		

CALCUDOKU №6

8×	8+		1-	6+
		20×		
5	10×		5+	1-
3		6×		
1			1-	

CALCUDOKU №7

7+		11+		10×	
6×		7+		2	
11+	7+		6×	8+	6
					4
5+		7+	19+		3×
10×					

FUTOSHIKI

FUTOSHIKI №2

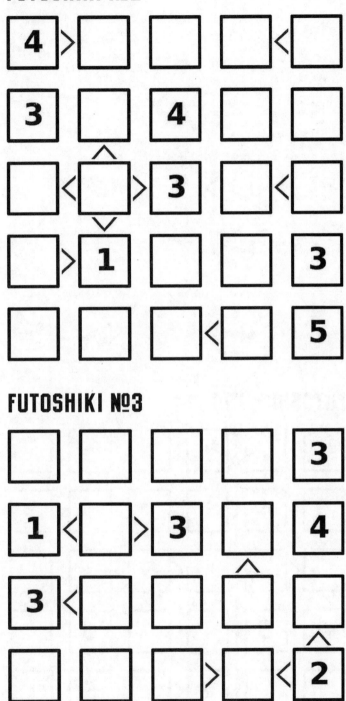

FUTOSHIKI №3

FUTOSHIKI №4

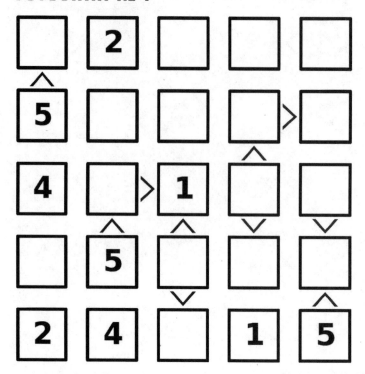

FUTOSHIKI №5

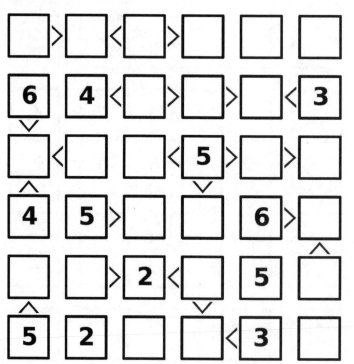

FUTOSHIKI №6

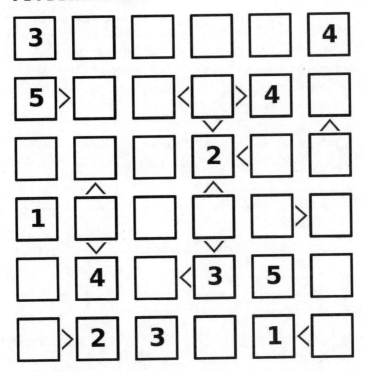

FUTOSHIKI №7

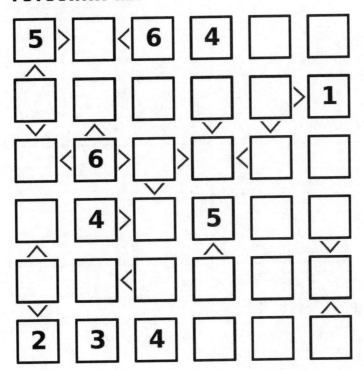

№ 2 CONSIGNMENTS IN AT ART'S GALLERY

Gallery owner Arthur Conasur recently returned from an international art fair and show, where he got commitments from four promising young artists to consign some of their works to him to sell through his gallery. The consigned works have already come in, and he is setting up the gallery to display them in a new show. Using the clues below, discover who the four artists are, their artistic specialties, and the price ranges at which they plan to offer their works at Art's show.

1. The group of young artists includes David Daring, who is not a sculptor; the woman who paints landscapes in watercolor; and the artist whose price range for the show will be $500–$1,000.

2. Pamela Primo has set a four-figure minimum for her works that will be on display, which are not oil-on-canvas still lifes.

3. Cynthia Studio won't have the smallest minimum price for her works, nor the highest. Evan Aesthete doesn't paint oils on canvas.

4. The oil-on-canvas still lifes are not being priced at either a minimum of $1,500 or a maximum of $1,500.

5. The artist pricing her works at between $1,500 and $2,500 doesn't paint watercolors or create mixed-media abstracts.

		Specialty				Price range			
		oils on canvas	watercolors	sculptures	mixed media	$500–$1,000	$600–$1,500	$1,500–$2,500	$2,000–$3,000
Artist	Cynthia Studio								
	David Daring								
	Evan Aesthete								
	Pamela Primo								
Price range	$500–$1,000								
	$600–$1,500								
	$1,500–$2,500								
	$2,000–$3,000								

№3 THE FISHING COMPETITION

Four friends who love to fish entered a bass-fishing competition and placed some bets among themselves as to which of them would be best at the competition's two challenges—biggest bass caught and the highest combined weight of four bass reeled in. As the competition concludes, see if you can figure out, based on the clues set out below, the weights each of our anglers registered in the two categories—and who won the bets. The results are going to be very close.

1. Fred's biggest fish did not weigh in at 4.85 pounds.

2. Hank's prize bass was not the smallest within the group, but Ian's best catch (which didn't weigh 4.52 pounds) outweighed Hank's.

3. Steve won the booby prize among the four for the lowest total weight of the four fish he turned in, but at least his biggest bass was not the least among them.

4. The combined weight of Hank's fish was not 14.59 pounds nor was his biggest fish 4.23 pounds; Ian's combined weight total was not 15.34 pounds.

5. The fisherman whose biggest catch was 4.08 pounds in weight didn't have a combined weight total of 15.17 or 15.34 pounds.

		Total weight				Biggest fish			
		14.11 lbs.	14.59 lbs.	15.17 lbs.	15.34 lbs.	4.08 lbs.	4.23 lbs.	4.52 lbs.	4.85 lbs.
Fisherman	Fred								
	Ian								
	Steve								
	Hank								
Biggest fish	4.08 lbs.								
	4.23 lbs.								
	4.52 lbs.								
	4.85 lbs.								

№4 OFFICE SPACE

JKR Commercial Real Estate Brokers landed a nice contract to find tenants to fill a new four-story office building. Rich Rawlins, the *R* of JKR, has had a good week implementing the contract—he has landed four tenants for the new building. Each of these tenants picked a different floor for their office suite. From the clues below, see if you can deduce which tenant will be on which floor with which amount of square footage.

1. Besides Smith & Jackson, CPAs, the group of new tenants includes the client who took 1,600 square feet (not on the first floor) for its office suite and the client that leased a suite on the second floor.

2. Peerless Employment Service is not leasing as much space as the CPA firm but more than the Eddlesten Insurance Agency.

3. Jackson & Smith, LLP, the law firm that Rich signed up as a tenant, won't be situated on the third floor nor have 1,000 square feet of office space in the building.

4. The first-floor suite that Rich just leased is 1,300 square feet in size.

5. The newly leased 2,000-square-foot office suite is not on the fourth floor, and the employment service did not take a 1,600-square-foot suite.

		Sq. footage				Floor			
		1,000 sq. ft.	1,300 sq. ft.	1,600 sq. ft.	2,000 sq. ft.	first	second	third	fourth
New tenant	CPAs								
	employment svc.								
	insurance								
	law firm								
Floor	first								
	second								
	third								
	fourth								

№5 FURNITURE DELIVERY

Claude delivers furniture for Cal's Furniture Mart. Today, he has four sofas to load onto his truck and deliver, each a different style and color. See if you can figure out, based on the information provided below, the color and price for each sofa.

1. Neither the sofa bed nor the traditional-style sofa Claude will deliver today is the least expensive or most expensive in the bunch.

2. The Victorian sofa being loaded on the truck is not gray and didn't cost $1,895, while the sofa bed, which isn't blue, cost $100 more than the sectional-modular sofa Claude is to deliver today.

3. Neither the beige nor the blue sofa sold for $1,895.

4. The traditional-style sofa is a shade of gray, and the dark gray sofa did not cost $2,095.

		Color				Price			
		beige	blue	light gray	dark gray	$1,895	$1,995	$2,095	$2,300
Sofa style	sectional								
	sofa bed								
	traditional								
	Victorian								
Price	$1,895								
	$1,995								
	$2,095								
	$2,300								

№6 FREIGHT TRAINS

Four long freight trains are bearing down on the Midwest City rail terminal, all scheduled to arrive this morning. The yardmaster needs to know how many "stack" cars (which haul freight containers stacked two-high on the car) and refrigerated box cars there are on the trains, so he can make sure sufficient gantry cranes will be available to off-load all the shipping containers and enough unloaders will be available to empty all the "reefer" cars quickly. Using the information provided below, see if you can help the yardmaster out by deducing how many stack cars and reefers are in each train.

1. Besides the first train to arrive this morning, there is the train pulling 68 stack cars and another train with 6 reefers.

2. Neither the third nor the fourth train scheduled to pull in today is a train with the fewest or second-fewest number of stack cars.

3. The third train has more reefers than the fourth train but less than the second train (which isn't pulling 55 stack cars).

4. The train that has 68 stack cars doesn't also have 14 reefers, and the train with 18 reefers doesn't have 55 stack cars.

		Stack cars				Reefers			
		55	60	65	68	6	12	14	18
Arrival	first								
	second								
	third								
	fourth								
Reefers	6								
	12								
	14								
	18								

CHAPTER 3
MEDIUM PUZZLES

CROSSWORD

ACROSS

1. Gable role
7. Fairy tale starter
11. Louisville Slugger
14. On dry land
15. Sign gas
16. NPR's ___ Shapiro
17. Prime minister, e.g.
19. Riddle-me-___
20. Went out, as a fire
21. Give a job to
22. Juicy fruit
23. Halvah ingredient
25. Ham, to Noah
26. Sharp slap
29. Father Brown's creator
33. Musical rattles
35. Little 'un
36. Masseur's workplace, maybe
37. Celestial
38. Rents out
40. Atlantic food fish
41. Luau souvenir
43. Suffering
44. Prepares to propose
47. "Duck soup!"
48. Stomach muscles, briefly
49. (Has) gotten up
51. Thermometer bottom
53. British king: Abbr.
54. "___-Voom!"
57. Absorbed, as a cost
58. Pay for something
61. Keep out
62. Scottish hillside
63. Coastal features
64. Checkup sounds
65. Places to overnight
66. Drunk, slangily

DOWN

1. Scrooge's cry
2. Secondhand
3. Bangkok native
4. Celestial guide for navigators
5. Eat away
6. Gridiron official, for short
7. Punctual
8. Closest at hand
9. ___ d'Azur (French Riviera)
10. 67.5 degrees on a compass: Init.
11. Watery expanse close to Norway and Russia named after a Dutch navigator
12. Field
13. Stadium level
18. Former Iranian rulers
22. ___ favor ("please," in Spanish)
24. Zodiac symbol
25. Passover feast
26. Sharp slap
27. Got shown
28. Gallery figures
30. Eagle's claws
31. Some tournaments
32. Spiteful
34. Telephones
39. Receptive (to)
42. Boise native
43. Chubby Checker's dance
45. Abate
46. Declaims
50. Word following "blessed" or "main"
51. ___ au rhum
52. Bryce Canyon state
53. Succotash ingredient
55. Penthouse feature
56. Old, in Germany
58. J. Edgar Hoover's org.: Init.
59. Towel stitching
60. "Acid"

№8 BODY LANGUAGE

1	2	3	4	5	6		7	8	9	10		11	12	13
14							15					16		
17					18							19		
	20					21					22			
		23		24					25					
26	27	28			29			30				31	32	
33			34				35				36			
37								38		39				
40			41		42		43							
44		45				46				47				
	48				49				50					
51	52			53					54		55	56		
57			58				59						60	
61			62				63							
64			65				66							

THINK ABOUT IT

Working on puzzles engages the prefrontal cortex of the brain, which is responsible for your highest-level cognitive functions—including those involved in planning, decision-making, and problem-solving. Some suggest that puzzles are an effective way to strengthen this area of your brain.

ACROSS

1. English singer who goes by her first name
6. Historical periods
10. Freeway exit
14. Secretary of Education under Trump
15. Canine visitor to Oz
16. Large jug
17. Newton or Stern
18. Catcall
19. "Cogito, _____ sum"
20. Beethoven's *Ode to Joy* work
23. Formal footwear
24. Green govt. agcy.
25. "Or else!" e.g.
28. Built
32. Bray starter
33. The common people in pre-Revolution France
36. Norway's patron saint
38. Fellows
39. Word following "wing" or "life"
40. It typically garners a silver medal
45. Der Spiegel article?
46. Main courses
47. Scarcely
49. Suffix with "Jud" or "And"
50. Beauty pageant coronet
52. Latest in an indefinitely numerous series
57. Crime boss
59. 401(k) alternatives
60. Between ports
61. Commotions
62. Regal address
63. Get a new tenant for
64. Desire
65. Dry run
66. Arduous journeys

DOWN

1. Score after deuce
2. He loved Lucy
3. *Dear _____ Hansen*
4. Abominate
5. Reversion of abandoned property to the state
6. High-octane gas no longer sold
7. Quarters
8. Crowning
9. "And that's that!"
10. Stages, as a historical battle
11. Amiss
12. *Family Guy* daughter
13. Debate position
21. Brother of Cain and Abel
22. Unlocks, to a bard
25. Not these
26. _____ of Troy
27. Change, chemically
28. *Giant* author Ferber
29. Recorded
30. Dot-commerce
31. Diner chain name
34. Little devils
35. Fam. member
37. Preeminent
41. Half-moon tide
42. Bridge and drilling expert
43. Confab
44. First woman to fly across the Atlantic
48. Dog used to hunt varmints
50. Eye drops
51. Atlas enlargement
52. _____ reflection
53. US-Canada border lake
54. Capri, for one
55. They shall inherit the earth, per the Psalms
56. Devours
57. Crow cry
58. 42-Down's org.

№9 ORDINALS

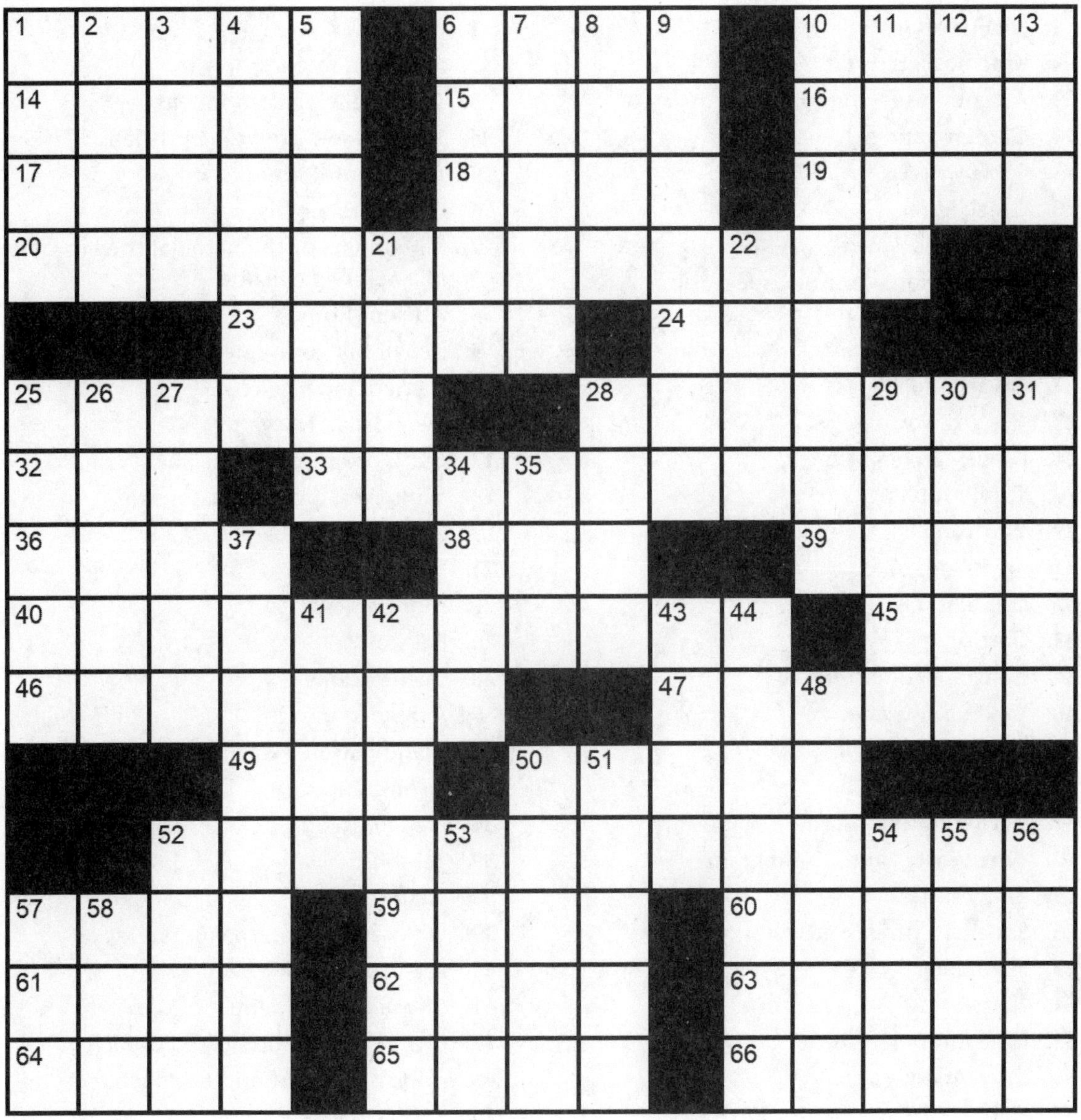

1970S TRIVIA CHALLENGE

What is the name of the supersonic passenger jet that England and France developed in the 1970s?

Name the blockbuster hit single that the English rock group Queen released in 1975.

ACROSS

1. Health resort
4. Kind of diver
9. Attention-seeking sounds
14. Garden pond fish
15. Fable writer
16. Greek letter
17. Indisposed
18. Compilation of outtakes featuring funny mistakes and mishaps
20. Dregs
22. Go around, bypass
23. "___ to worry"
24. Dogie-catching rope
27. Total drubbing
29. Way too high, as an asking price
31. Bucks and does
32. Lion's home
33. Getting ____ years
34. Contract conditions
35. Kind of insurance
36. Biblical prophet
38. Quick-witted
41. Gathering clouds, say
42. "The Waste Land" monogram
45. Zingy taste
46. Southern African gazelles
49. Halted legally
51. "Rats!"
52. "The Purloined Letter" author
53. Consumed
55. Henry VIII's second or fourth
56. Closest advisors . . . or a description of each set of shaded squares
60. *Wheel of Fortune* buy
61. What some dress to, with "the"
62. Dabbling ducks
63. Jewel
64. Frighten
65. Dutch cheeses
66. Hesitant sounds

DOWN

1. Adept
2. Medieval weapon
3. Airplane wing component
4. Sat. for Jews, Sun. for Christians
5. Animation frame
6. Hangouts for GIs
7. Bibliophile, or the name of the library cop in a *Seinfeld* episode
8. Ancient Rome's _____ Way
9. Repair bill component
10. Camera type, briefly
11. Two-Oscar Tracy
12. Math proposition
13. Winter road crews, at times
19. Beginning for "while"
21. "Dear" one
25. More or less
26. Hue
28. Citrus drinks
30. Acapulco uncle
34. Island nation east of Fiji
35. Jason's ship
36. French friend
37. Patch up
38. Loafers, e.g.
39. Of a certain fraternal organization
40. Pre-cable need
41. Chose from a menu
42. Measure of a ship's cargo capacity
43. Principal of Bart and Lisa's school
44. Respects and admires
46. "Blank check" type of co. favored by some on Wall St.
47. Diminutive
48. Bikini top
50. Intrinsically: Lat.
54. March Madness org.
57. Always, to the versifier
58. Advanced legal deg.
59. Serpentine letter

№10 EMBEDDED ENTRIES

1	2	3	■	4	5	6	7	8	■	9	10	11	12	13
14			■	15					■	16				
17			■	18					19					
20			21	■	22				■			23		
24			25	26	■	27				28				
29					30			■	31					
32			33				■	34						
■		35					36	37			■			
38	39	40			■	41				42	43	44		
45			■	46	47				48					
49			50				51							
52			53			54		55						
56		57				58	59		60					
61				■	62			■	63					
64				■	65			■	66					

DID YOU KNOW?

The standards for American-style crosswords (like those in this book) include one that says that the black squares in the puzzle grid must be laid out in what is called 180-degree rotational, or radial, symmetry. That is, if you turn the puzzle upside down by rotating it 180 degrees, the pattern of black and white squares looks the same. Why is this expected? The only answers I have are (i) that is the way they always have been designed and (ii) it makes the puzzle more visually appealing.

ACROSS

1. Ottoman title
6. Musher's transport
10. _____ of Capri
14. Tavern perch
15. Prod
16. Warm, so to speak
17. Difficult tee shots for an IT specialist?
19. Triumphant cry
20. "Chances ___"
21. *A Chorus Line* number
22. Storage area
24. Attractive or appealing in appearance
27. Moor
28. Nickname for a golfer who constantly pulls the ball left into the rough?
32. Rose Parade vehicles
35. What Leary tripped on
36. Genetic initials
37. Lummoxes
38. US soldiers
39. Fencing swords
41. Actor's rep.
42. Lowe or Reiner
43. Comes up
44. Lament of a golfer who missed a putt that would have given her an under-par score on the hole?
48. Harness parts
49. It's 8,849 meters high
53. Fine fur
55. Start of a vowel sequence
56. Map abbr.
57. _____ synthesizer
58. Default choice of the golfer who can't decide which club to use?
62. Cogitate
63. Busy as _____
64. Display, wear
65. ABA membs.
66. Off-color
67. Does a valet's job

DOWN

1. "Phooey!"
2. Electronic game pioneer
3. Existentialist Kierkegaard
4. Mason's tray
5. Munic. official
6. Small piano
7. Hold dear
8. Barely get, with "out"
9. Move downward
10. Entirely
11. Places to find shells
12. Put on board, as cargo
13. Part of QED
18. Frolics
23. "Well, ___-di-dah!"
25. "Beat it!"
26. Feed bag contents
27. Snake's warning
29. Used to prove that the defendant couldn't have done it
30. "Trick" joint
31. Back talk
32. Exercise target
33. Sluggish
34. Farthest from the center
38. Oodles
39. Canal of song
40. Docking spot
42. Subscriber's extension
43. Ibuprofen brand
45. Light brown shades
46. Yang's opposite
47. Reduced, as a sail
50. Miscue
51. Baby bird?
52. Bivouac sights
53. Jane Austen novel
54. Defeat decisively
55. Not many
59. Half a sawbuck
60. Sixth sense, for short
61. Hoppy brew, briefly

№11 GOLF IS A DIFFICULT GAME

1	2	3	4	5		6	7	8	9		10	11	12	13
14						15					16			
17					18						19			
20					21				22	23				
24			25	26				27						
			28				29						30	31
32	33	34				35					36			
37					38				39	40				
41				42				43						
44			45	46			47							
		48					49				50	51	52	
53	54					55					56			
57				58	59				60	61				
62				63					64					
65				66					67					

THINK ABOUT IT

Your short-term memory stores information for a few seconds. Scientists used to think that people could store between five and nine items in their short-term memory, but more recent research suggests we can hold up to four informational "chunks" (groups of items encoded as a single unit—think the segments of a phone number) in our short-term memory.

ACROSS

1. Unlikely to bite
5. Colorado ski center
10. Woodworking groove
14. Pinnacle
15. Stiller's comedy partner
16. "In your dreams!"
17. Music legend who recorded "Georgia on My Mind"
19. Common contraction
20. Church dignitary
21. Assert without proof
23. Swagger
24. Famed playwright and screenwriter
27. Count (on)
29. Cotillion girl, briefly
30. Electrical current unit
33. Toper
35. Whole bunch
38. ___ constrictor
39. Creator of Spider-Man and Ant-Man
42. Swelled head
43. Apple leftover
45. Victorian, for one
46. Heavy hammer
48. Santa ___ (city in California)
50. Kind of cracker
52. The "Piano Man"
55. Oklahoma city
59. Connected to the internet
60. Artist's studio
62. Lyric poems
63. Head writer for two hit TV comic series
66. Lean, list
67. Easy two-pointer
68. Fork feature
69. Company with toy fuel trucks
70. "Naughty you!"
71. First family's home

DOWN

1. Protective covers for infields
2. Separated from one another
3. Football coach Urban _____
4. Rule out
5. Latin 101 verb
6. Tranquil
7. Buddy
8. Bard's "before"
9. Vocally twangy
10. Some newspapers
11. Got together
12. Wild Australian dog
13. More than occasionally
18. "_____ Gonna Hate"
22. Hallucinogenic initials
25. Trap
26. Teen fave
28. Davidson or Buttigieg
30. Epitomy of easiness
31. Pasture sound
32. Is analogous to
34. TV host-turned-New Age musician
36. When it's on your face, that's bad
37. Misery
40. Cornstarch brand
41. Jubilant
44. Enrolls (in the armed forces)
47. Copy
49. Author ___ Rand
51. Shakespearean warning signal
52. Diner seating choice
53. Not a big-studio film
54. Solidifies
56. Hopping mad
57. Île de la Cité locale
58. As You Like It forest
61. Use a keyboard
64. Sound made at a doctor's request
65. Deep-pile Scandinavian rug

№12 ON A FIRST-NAME BASIS

1980S TRIVIA CHALLENGE

Who was the English Prime Minister throughout the 1980s? Hint: Her nickname was "Iron Lady."

Marty McFly and Doc Brown were the two main characters in what 1985 hit movie?

ACROSS

1. Forgoes food
6. Recede
9. Eateries that serve lots of flapjacks, briefly
14. The *U* in UHF
15. Barley brew
16. Less dated
17. Go bad
18. Beluga yield
19. Fruit-flavored soft drink brand
20. Space rock visible as it burns up on entering the earth's atmosphere
23. Jabber
24. Driver's lic. and others
25. Call for
29. Floral necklace
30. Rough cousin of 31-Down
32. Ending for cant, concert, or czar
33. Space rocks that orbit the sun
37. Roughly
39. Goulash
40. Tarnish
42. Touched down
43. Looks after
45. Space rock that survives its passage through the earth's atmosphere and hits the ground
47. "___ got it!"
48. Dana perfume brand
50. Gorilla
51. Comeback
53. Refrain syllable
54. Mornings, for short
57. Space snowball of ice and dust that periodically approaches (and becomes visible from) the earth, named after the astronomer who first decribed it
61. Briny expanse
64. Melber or Fleischer
65. Humor with a twist
66. Squirrel away
67. Pewter component
68. Not relaxed
69. A group's binding customs and conventions
70. High school subj.
71. Hatha and Bikram, for two

DOWN

1. Persnickety
2. Omega's opposite
3. Bend down
4. The Kingston ____
5. More briny
6. Brings in
7. It's kept up with posts
8. Spelling contests
9. Spanish princess
10. Center, core
11. Fess (up)
12. Teacher's favorite
13. Mexican Mrs.
21. Blockhead
22. Gymnast's goal
26. Garlicky sauce
27. Arctic native
28. Coffeehouse order
29. Bawdy
30. French farewell
31. "____ It Romantic?"
33. Out of bed and moving around
34. Martin, Carell, or Jobs
35. Article of faith
36. Metrical foot
38. Unadorned
41. Lacerates
44. Leaves in the lurch
46. Opaqueness
49. The Braves, on scoreboards
52. Chicago hub
53. Pulling even with
54. Honor _____ thieves
55. The brainy bunch
56. Eyelid problems
58. After curfew
59. "____ go bragh!"
60. Popular cookie brand
61. Resistance unit
62. Bill's partner in love
63. Musical aptitude

№13 LOOK UP IN THE SKY

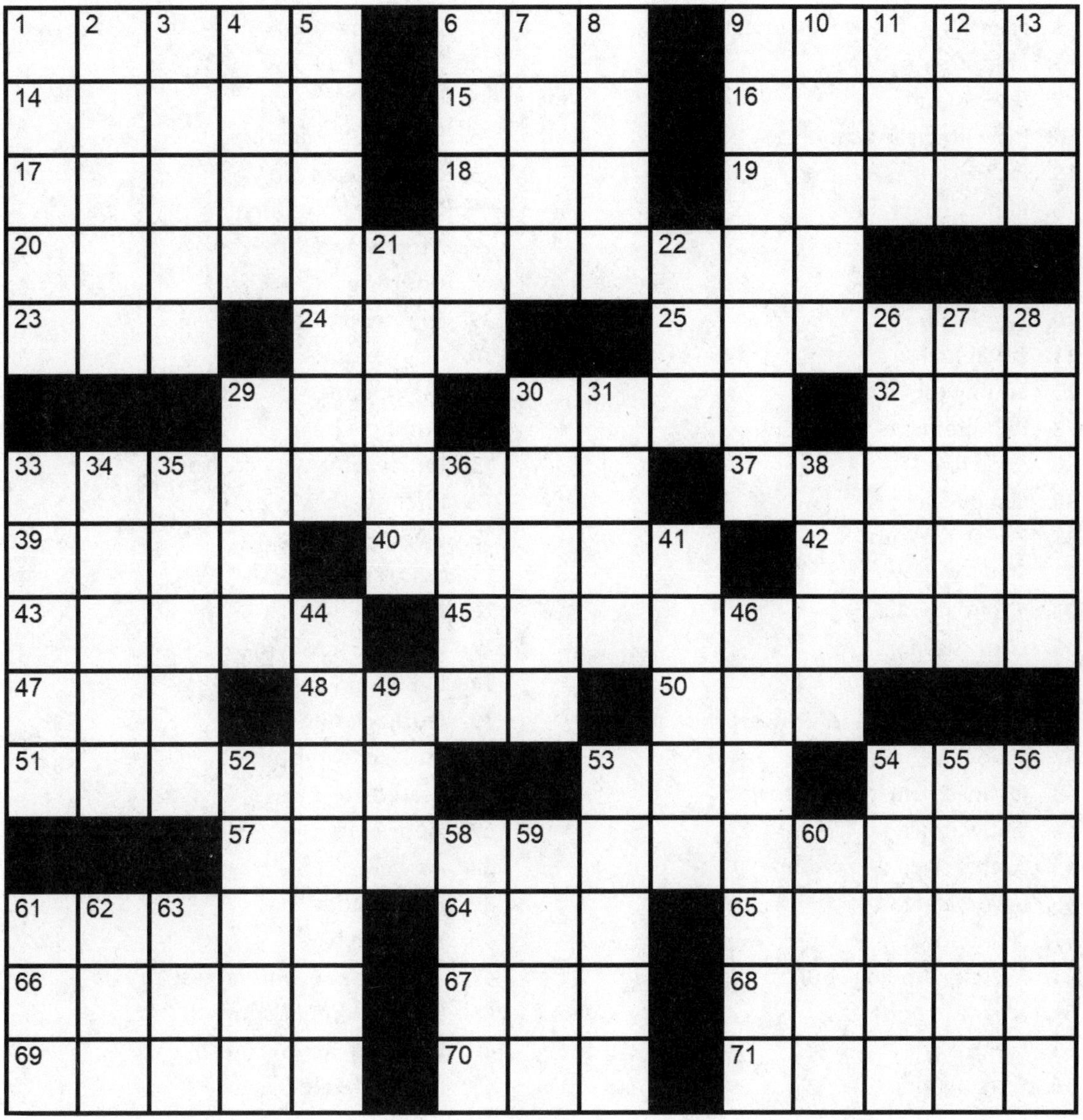
1 2 3 4 5 6 7 8 9 10 11 12 13
14 15 16
17 18 19
20 21 22
23 24 25 26 27 28
29 30 31 32
33 34 35 36 37 38
39 40 41 42
43 44 45 46
47 48 49 50
51 52 53 54 55 56
57 58 59 60
61 62 63 64 65
66 67 68
69 70 71

DID YOU KNOW?

Sudoku did not originate in Japan. It was created by an American, Howard Garns, in 1979 and was called "Number Place." The puzzle was introduced to Japan in 1984 and became a big hit there under the Japanese name "Sudoku," which literally translates to "number single." A few years later, it migrated from Japan back to the US as "Sudoku."

ACROSS

1. Have _____ (be well connected)
5. Epic story
9. Can't stand
14. New Rochelle school
15. Isn't wrong?
16. Repetitive practice
17. Baseball superstar
19. Ming things
20. ___ Amin
21. Fossil fuel
22. Ending for Oktober
23. Requirements
25. Shoe liner
30. Gaudy
32. Poetic measure
33. Sleep acronym
34. *The Matrix* hero
35. Educ. support grp.
36. Place, stead
37. *Lavender Mist* and *Convergence*, for two
42. "Poor me!"
43. Japanese ornamental carp
44. Chow down
45. Archipelago unit: Abbr.
46. Savory spread
47. "Pipe down!"
51. Sketchy funding source
54. Japanese port
55. Lambs' cries
56. Corn serving
58. Impair the appearance of
59. Growl
61. Famous singer who got his big break with NSYNC
64. Sultan's wives, as a group
65. White House staffer
66. Sheltered, nautically
67. Not quite right
68. Oaf
69. Clutter

DOWN

1. Intending
2. "Not a clue!"
3. Blacker
4. Highlands negative
5. Delhi dress
6. Garlicky condiment
7. African antelope
8. Court fig.
9. "-ly" word, usually
10. Copper-zinc alloy
11. Memorable
12. Bullring cheer
13. Initials of Jekyll's creator
18. Pitches
22. Ewes and hens, e.g.
24. Soft tennis shots
26. More chilly
27. Defense acronym
28. Onion kin
29. Outback birds
31. Turkish water pipes
36. Seated yoga pose
37. Hoosegow
38. As well
39. Fried squid
40. Part of n.b.
41. Pakistan's second-largest city
46. Old Testament songs
48. Steamed Tex-Mex dish
49. Imperial edicts
50. Analyzes syntactically
52. Nostrils
53. Samurai's martial art
57. Got 100 on
59. Doo-wop syllable
60. *China Beach* setting
61. Fond du ___, Wisc.
62. Trouble, afflict
63. "Kapow!"

1	2	3	4		5	6	7	8		9	10	11	12	13
14					15					16				
17				18						19				
20				21				22						
23			24			25	26	27				28	29	
30					31		32				33			
			34				35			36			
37	38	39			40			41					
42				43			44						
45				46				47			48	49	50
51			52			53		54					
		55				56	57			58			
59	60				61	62			63				
64				65				66					
67				68				69					

THINK ABOUT IT

Getting a good night's sleep is important to maintaining brain health. Without sleep, the pathways in your brain that let you learn and create new memories are degraded; and, according to recent studies, sleep enables your brain to clear out toxins that accumulate while you are awake.

№8 COLORFUL COLORS

```
A I S H C U F Y Y O O H E V G
T E N O O R A M D G C O C I J
W C E O M A G E N T A T U O E
M O U A Z U R E U U X P P L M
A E L P R U P S G B I I K E U
U K B L L E N I R E G N A T L
V L Y D E W Y O U E I K A K P
E I V O R Y N U B W V U J L K
S L A T L Z Y Q I R P L A J C
I A N A E I S R S E E V I K A
R C R A N A E U A G E B R S L
E O V D L P L T C N K D M J B
C R I M S O N M D A A D A A T
A G O L D M G E A R B C E J E
O N A E L U R E C O C H R E J
```

AMBER	FUCHSIA	MAGENTA	PURPLE
AZURE	GOLD	MAROON	SALMON
BRONZE	HOT PINK	MAUVE	SILVER
BURGUNDY	INDIGO	NAVY BLUE	TANGERINE
CANARY YELLOW	IVORY	OCHRE	TAUPE
CERISE	JADE	ORANGE	TEAL
CERULEAN	JET BLACK	PERIWINKLE	TURQUOISE
CORAL	LAVENDER	PLUM	VIOLET
CRIMSON	LILAC	PUCE	

№9 COMMODITIES TRADED ON EXCHANGES

```
R L I O E D U R C A T T L E D
D I P S O Y B E A N S T A O A
R C C O R N J V L O N A H T E
M U N E D B Y L O M P G E N L
E H B I P S V I P R O P A N E
W C O B Z A B S Q L L T T C Y
M H I G E E L X D A U I I O O
U E E U S R N L T R P K N P A
I E L A J O W I A A Y L G P J
N F Q I T E N L L D C I O E C
I F U T R U G M E O I M I R O
M O O E M A O N L K S U L A B
U C B N S I C T A O C A M G A
L M P I L U M B E R O I G U L
A N U T P L U P D O O W N S T
```

ALUMINIUM
AMBER
CATTLE
COBALT
COFFEE
COPPER
CORN
COTTON
CRUDE OIL
ETHANOL

GASOLINE
GOLD
HEATING OIL
HOGS
LEAD
LUMBER
MILK
MOLYBDENUM
NATURAL GAS
NICKEL

OATS
ORANGE JUICE
PALLADIUM
PALM OIL
PLATINUM
PROPANE
RICE
RUBBER
SILVER
SOYBEANS

SUGAR
TIN
WHEAT
WOOD PULP
WOOL
ZINC

Nº10 ITALY'S 32 LARGEST CITIES PLUS 2

```
A K Q M I L A N S A S S A R I
I K O R H N W H Q A B O V A X
C R O N G Q F Q L I T M I K I
S M E O R M F E C N E R O L F
E J L G N O R E A A B E K W V
R O P A G N V R T A T L Z N P
B V S G O I A I L S A A A I A
N I I A O T O A L I E P N N R
P A R A N F C E G O L I E I M
R O A S N O E U M E M D R E A
A N I B I N R R S I O D S T N
T E L G J E E R M L S Q U I
O G G X P G N V V A I I Z R T
V E A P A D U A A N R L A I A
R E C I N E V B A R I A R N L
```

BARI (9)

BOLOGNA (7)

BRESCIA (16)

CAGLIARI (26)

CATANIA (10)

FERRARA (30)

FLORENCE (8)

FOGGIA (28)

GENOA (6)

LATINA (31)

LIVORNO (25)

MESSINA (13)

MILAN (2)

MODENA (19)

NAPLES (3)

PADUA (14)

PALERMO (5)

PARMA (17)

PERUGIA (23)

PISA (55)

PRATO (19)

RAVENNA (24)

REGGIO CALABRIA
  (21)

REGGIO EMILIA (22)

RIMINI (27)

ROME (1)

SALERNO (29)

SASSARI (32)

SIENA (129)

TARANTO (18)

TRIESTE (15)

TURIN (4)

VENICE (12)

VERONA (11)

№11 T-FORMATION

```
Y T I L A T O T C C V E T O T Z T
T E E T C A R T T A T I X S A U R
T L T N P R E T T U T S E A T E J
A E L A T E L T T A T T T T T F H
T W P T T A T A A T T R I T I O N
    D U O S T T F A A F I E T
    W T T S E I E J R W D M A
    V O G T T T V U T U G P T
    R R T T O T T E T K F T A
    E D E Z O T T I I A M G T
    T S N T I O T M E O T N A
    T W E X M T A E T T V S R
    O M T A A T I T R A T E Z
    R L T M A H O R Y T S A T
    T O D T U A T H G I T S L
```

ATTEMPT	RAT-A-TAT	TENET	TOTTER
ATTEST	STATUETTE	TENTATIVE	TROTTER
ATTITUDE	STATUTE	TESTATE	TUTOR
ATTRACT	STUTTER	TIGHT	TUTTI-FRUTTI
ATTRITION	TASTY	TITRATE	TWITTER
FITTEST	TATAMI	TOMATO	WATT
LATTE	TATTLETALE	TOTALITY	
MOTTO	TATTY	TOTE	
PUTT	TAUT	TOTEM	

№12 VOWEL-APALOOZA

```
L A E O S A I N A E C O D A I
O I E I R E E I L O O C L O I
S D H R R U M A U I I I I N E
O A O O Y E T A U Q E D A N I
R P I T D N A I E N U U O J A
E E T A I V A J E A G A U L I
A M C R G G U E Q U E U E O E
F A I O O N U O R A R E T T P
E N X E E Y O A I A T A A I O
E O A A N D T P E B S I I O I
U M U I O E O U E R T E B A S
C I B O L T G A A I U P A I S
A E V L U O N U N E N B R C A
V E O I A I E I E P B Q A L C
E A D I E U K A I R O H P U E
```

ACADEMIA	A-ONE	COOLIE	IOTA
ADIEU	ARABIA	EERIE	JUNEAU
AEOLIAN	AUDIO	EUGENE	MAUI
AERIE	AVIATE	EUPHORIA	OCEANIA
AEROSOL	BEANIE	EVACUEE	ORATORIO
AIDA	BEAUTY	GAIA	QUEUE
AIOLI	BUREAU	IAGO	TIBIA
ALEE	CAESAREAN	INADEQUATE	UTOPIA
ALIENEE	CASSIOPEIA	INAUGURATE	VOODOO
ANOMIE	CIAO	INITIATE	

№13 WORDS WE'VE BORROWED FROM THE FRENCH

```
F U O D L T E R A B A C I H C
S A K M S E L P E T E Y E E G
G E A G E O T Y E L T N D A B
D R A V E L U O B R I A S I J
L U C U I C E P H H C T C B U
I B A R N A H T C A R N E H R
S G D I R E T A F O U Y C J E
N E E C W E M I N D O R N U L
E V T O H W T O O D T E A B U
T K L C O I M S S N E L I I C
U Y I H R Y S G I B D L F L I
Y L Z E B I A Z A C P A I E D
C V P T E H E R I T A G E E I
X A A R E S D A L A S I O L R
Z W F N T J M R O L E H C A B
```

APERITIF
ATTACHE
AVIATION
BACHELOR
BOULEVARD
BUREAU
CABARET
CADET
CHANDELIER

CHIC
CLICHE
CREPE
DETOUR
DOSSIER
ELITE
FACADE
FIANCE
GALLERY

GASTRONOMY
HERITAGE
HOTEL
JUBILEE
LIAISON
MACHINE
MENU
NAVY
OMELET

RICOCHET
RIDICULE
SALAD
SOUP
UTENSIL
ZEST

№14 FAMOUS INVENTORS

```
T A T J J R E J S K G G O L L E K
L E L I O L D S M U C D S S R B N
D U S E E F U L T O N N H E A H I
F N M L S H R E Q O O C I K T Z L
K A F I A E N A N S U R R I N T K
A E R F E B I E I A R I M E E R N
I M R A E R V D R A M S B S J E A
N R I R D R E S C H I T R E S H R
Z I G N E A M Z J A A O S I L D F
O P L S B U Y I N T M F T A D L L
W A E W R I G H T B R O T H E R S
T S B O O T R A K W D R A D D O G
E T O R X J T D D A V I N C I O J
Y E N T I H W A S K T P C K L A S
H U F H E P S R W E U L A C S A P
D R G R F F D R A E Y D O O G D F
I N O C R A M W V K R E E V B O G
```

BELL (telephone)
BENZ (automobile)
BIRDSEYE (flash freezing)
CARRIER (air conditioner)
CRISTOFORI (piano)
DA VINCI (parachute)
DAGUERRE (first photograph)
DIESEL (diesel engine)
EASTMAN (roll film)
EDISON (phonograph)
EVINRUDE (outboard motor)
FAHRENHEIT (thermometer)
FARADAY (electric motor)

FARNSWORTH (TV)
FERMI (nuclear reactor)
FRANKLIN (bifocals)
FULTON (steamboat)
GODDARD (liquid fuel rocket)
GOODYEAR (vulcanized rubber)
GUTENBERG (movable type)
HERTZ (concept of radar)
KELLOGG (cornflakes)
LUMIERE (color photography)
MARCONI (radio)
MORSE (Morse code)
NAISMITH (basketball)

NOBEL (dynamite)
OLDS (assembly line)
OTIS (elevator)
PASCAL (first calculator)
PASTEUR (pasteurization)
SALK (polio vaccine)
TESLA (induction motor)
VOLTA (batteries)
WATT (modern steam engine)
WHITNEY (cotton gin)
WOZNIAK (Apple I computer)
WRIGHT BROTHERS (airplane)

CRYPTOGRAM

№8 CONTRADICTION

QCEHTK HBV BHNFGTHU HTFEHUK JQG HUJHRK UGKV

_____

NQVFB NVEWVBK JQVT NQVR HBV XHUUVP CWGT NG

_____

HXN FT HXXGBPHTXV JFNQ NQV PFXNHNVK GM BVHKGT.

_____

—GKXHB JFUPV

_____

HINTS (SEE PAGE 124): 9, 15

№9 THE SOURCE OF BRILLIANCE

BJSAPJC M UQKAL RJOCJJ QK SBAJUUSOJBIJ BQC

_____

SHMOSBMASQB BQC YQAP AQOJAPJC OQ AQ APJ

_____

HMESBO QK OJBSNV. UQDJ, UQDJ, UQDJ, APMA SV APJ

_____

VQNU QK OJBSNV.

_____

—XQUKOMBO MHMRJNV HQWMCA

_____

HINTS (SEE PAGE 124): 8, 34

№10 DESTINY CALLED

WH WTFRNC DPVK FT WN, "VS HTM PCN P DTZKVNC,

_____

HTM OVZZ JNUTWN P LNINCPZ. VS HTM PCN P WTIB,

_____

HTM OVZZ JNUTWN FRN ETEN." VIDFNPK, V OPD P

_____

EPVIFNC, PIK JNUPWN EVUPDDT.

_____

—EPJZT EVUPDDT

_____

HINTS (SEE PAGE 124): 32, 37

№11 A LITTLE HUMILITY IS IN ORDER

KPJB EVM QJA AV LJ GHJXNUJBA, APJHJ WHJ WDD

_____

APVXJ APNBQX, APJ PVBVHX, APJ AKJBAE–VBJ QMB

_____

XWDMAJX, WDD APVXJ APNBQX. EVM PWOJ AV HJIJILJH

_____

NA NXB'A TVH EVM, NA'X TVH APJ GHJXNUJBFE.

_____

—PWHHE X. AHMIWB

_____

HINTS (SEE PAGE 124): 2, 27

№12 DISTINGUISHING CHARACTERISTIC

BFW LFGXW PVAAWDWIUW TWBLWWI UGIOBDEUBVGI

_____

MIP UDWMBVGI VO WNMUBXK BFVO: BFMB M BFVIY

_____

UGIOBDEUBWP UMI GIXK TW XGJWP MABWD VB VO

_____

UGIOBDEUBWP; TEB M BFVIY UDWMBWP VO XGJWP

_____

TWAGDW VB WNVOBO.

_____

—UFMDXWO PVUQWIO

_____

HINTS (SEE PAGE 124): 7, 21

№13 THE VALUE OF SHARED MIRTH

JHP RPXFCV NXMIR CJIPCRPF ODNN KFDHI PHPTDPG

_____

DHCJ X ENJGPF EJTTMHDJH JL RPXFC CRXH RJMFG

_____

GBPHC JH KJCR GDUPG DH DHOXFU OFPGCNDHI ODCR

_____

CRP TPHCXN UPTJH JL MHERXFDCXKNP LPPNDHI.

_____

—ODNNDXT AXTPG

_____

HINTS (SEE PAGE 124): 10, 26

SUDOKU

SUDOKU №8

3			1	6			5	
		7	4	8				
						6	9	
		6				9		
1	3						7	8
		2				1		
	6	3						
				5	8	7		
	4			9	1			3

SUDOKU №9

5		8			3	7		
	2			7				6
	9		5					
	3			2				
1	4	2				5	8	7
				8			9	
					7		1	
7				1			3	
		4	3			8		5

SUDOKU №10

		4			9		2	
			2			1		8
2		7	8			4	5	
		3	5	6				
	9					3		
			9	3	6			
	7	6			4	5		2
4		1			5			
	8		6			3		

SUDOKU №11

2	8			7	6		4	9
			9		3			6
		3						2
7	5				9			
	4					6		
			3				2	5
5						2		
1			6		7			
8	3		2	9			1	4

SUDOKU №12

	5	9			1			6
7						1	4	
			2		6			
		8	1				6	
	4	2				3	1	
	3				9	7		
			9		2			
	9	7						5
6			3			9	8	

SUDOKU №13

7			6				4	
	5		4	7	3	6	1	
								9
			9	6		5		1
8		5		3	4			
5								
	7	8	5	4	1		2	
	4				9			6

SUDOKU №14

			9			8		
	4	6		2	1		9	
	8			3	4	2		
								9
2	7						8	6
1								
		5	3	4			1	
	6		1	9		5	3	
		7			8			

SUDOKU №15

5			6					3
				9	3			
6		1	4				9	
4		7			6		1	
		3				4		
	6		8			3		7
	9				5	8		2
			2	7				
7					9			6

CALCUDOKU №8

8+	6+		15×		1
	6	8+		30×	7+
15×					
60×		11+		1	7+
	5+	30×		8×	
1			3		6

CALCUDOKU №9

8+	12+		1	12×	5×
		12×			
7+	4+	180×		4	8×
				5×	
12+		6+	4		54×
	5		2		

CALCUDOKU №10

8×	5	3×	24×	3+	
	60×			8+	
7+			7+		108×
	4	7+			
8+	4+	4	8+		
		6		6+	

CALCUDOKU №11

5×	12×	20×	18×		24×
4	20×	3 :		6	12×
1-		2	5 :		
	13+		2 :	9+	5×
6					

CALCUDOKU №12

60×		5+		3 :	1-
	40×		6×		
1		6		20×	7+
0-		2	5-		
	4×	15×		2×	
4			60×		

CALCUDOKU №13

5-		2	4+	11+	
1-		30×			7+
24×	1		14+		
		4×		8+	
3-			3-		6 :
5	6×		4×		

FUTOSHIKI №8

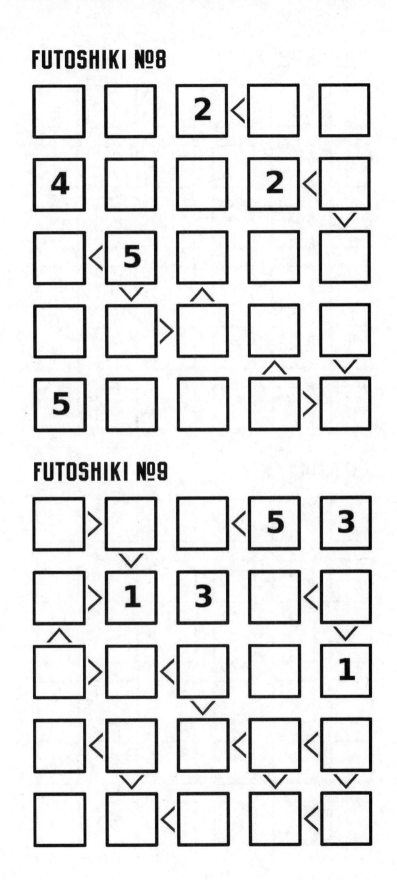

FUTOSHIKI №9

FUTOSHIKI №10

FUTOSHIKI №11

FUTOSHIKI №12

FUTOSHIKI №13

№7 MIKE, THE AUTO MECHANIC

Mike, the auto mechanic, has a large and loyal clientele because he really knows what he is doing and is reliable and trustworthy. Early this morning, four of his customers showed up at his shop with car issues they needed him to address. Based on the clues below, see if you can align the customers, their cars, and the problems Mike has to address and figure out the order in which he plans to work on the cars.

1. Between the 2018 Ford Mike will be working on today and the car that has the "check engine" light on, one is third in line to be worked on and the other is John's car.

2. One of the guys brought in the 2016 Volvo, but he is not looking for 30,000-mile service on the vehicle. Jim's car, which is not the 2019 Subaru, needs the brakes relined.

3. John isn't the first or last in line to get his car (which is not the 2016 Volvo) worked on today, but he will have to wait until after Janice's car is serviced.

4. Joe, who doesn't own the 2020 Chevy, is getting new tires and his wheels aligned.

5. Janice's car, which doesn't have the "check engine" light issue, is not a 2019 Subaru. Joe's car is not the 2018 Ford.

		Model of car				Work needed				Order of work			
		2016 Volvo	2018 Ford	2019 Subaru	2020 Chevy	engine light	brake job	30K service	new tires	first	second	third	fourth
Customer	Janice												
	Jim												
	John												
	Joe												
Order of work	first												
	second												
	third												
	fourth												
Work needed	engine light												
	brake job												
	30K service												
	new tires												

№ 8 RATING WEATHER FORECASTERS

Middletown's weekly newspaper is rating the accuracy of the three main sources for Middletown weather forecasts—WeatherInfo.com, local Channel 2/XTRZ TV, and local KGXZ radio—by comparing their Friday forecasts for Saturday's weather (which included some rain) against the actual weather data for Saturday gleaned from the Federal Weather Service (FWS) files. The review compares each forecast to FWS data in three critical categories: high temperature, highest wind on that day, and how much rain fell. The FWS data vary slightly from the forecasts in each metric. Using the clues set out below, see if you can figure out what the FWS data show for each category and which forecast comes closest to the FWS data in each category.

1. One forecast said that the high temperature on Saturday would hit 91 degrees, another that the highest wind velocity would be 8 miles per hour that day, and the third called for ½ inch of rain.

2. The forecast that said the rain would be ¼ inch did not predict a high temperature of 93.

3. The Channel 2/XTRZ forecast didn't predict ⅛ inch of rain or a high wind of 12 or 15 miles per hour, but its wind prediction was higher than that of KGXZ, which predicted the day's high temperature to hit 90.

4. The forecast that called for Saturday rain totaling ⅓ of an inch also included a high temperature prediction 2 degrees higher than another forecast.

5. The actual FWS data do not show a high Saturday temperature of 89 or a high wind of 12 miles per hour; WeatherInfo.com didn't predict a high temperature of 89 either.

		High temp				Top wind				Rain amount			
		89 degrees	90 degrees	91 degrees	93 degrees	8 mph	10 mph	12 mph	15 mph	1/8 inch	1/4 inch	1/3 inch	1/2 inch
Data source	WeatherInfo												
	Channel 2												
	KGXZ radio												
	FWS												
Rain amount	1/8 inch												
	1/4 inch												
	1/3 inch												
	1/2 inch												
Top wind	8 mph												
	10 mph												
	12 mph												
	15 mph												

№9 BIRD-WATCHING

The Birding Club has an annual challenge in which teams see how many bird species they can identify in 24 hours. To get ready for this big event, four club members held a practice session at a state park, where each went off on a separate trail to see how many species they could spot on their own in three hours. And, while they were at it, they assisted the club in its efforts to inventory the two most populous species in the area, the northern cardinal and the American robin, by counting how many of those birds they spotted too. Try to use the clues below to find out who spotted and identified the most species of birds on their rambles and how many robin and cardinal sightings each had as well.

1. Bernie sighted more cardinals than Bonnie but less than the person who spotted 6 robins.

2. Neither of the two women who participated in the practice session could claim the most or least robin sightings among the group.

3. Bonnie spotted and identified 15 species of birds that day but didn't spot 6 robins or 2 cardinals.

4. Bert didn't spot 7 robins; Bernie didn't spot and identify 21 bird species.

5. Brenda didn't spot and identify 25 bird species, and Bonnie didn't spot 4 cardinals.

6. The one who spotted 7 robins didn't spot and identify 21 or 25 bird species.

		Species				Cardinals				Robins			
		15	19	21	25	2	3	4	5	3	4	6	7
Birder	Bernie												
	Bert												
	Bonnie												
	Brenda												
Robins	3												
	4												
	6												
	7												
Cardinals	2												
	3												
	4												
	5												

№10 THE HOT DOG CART

The city just awarded Harry a license to sell hot dogs, snacks, and soft drinks from a portable hot dog cart at the city park. The park is huge; with tons of traffic all year except the coldest days, the park is an ideal location for his little business. The next step for Harry was to figure out where in the park to position his cart to maximize sales. So, early in the summer, Harry set up business in four different spots in the park for a day to see how sales did in each spot. Based on the information set out below, can you deduce the revenue (rounded to the nearest $10) that Harry generated from the sale of hot dogs, snacks, and soft drinks, respectively, in each spot he tried out?

1. The spots Harry tried out included the softball/soccer fields, another spot that produced $340 in daily hot dog sales, a third spot where daily revenue from snacks came to $190, and a fourth location that generated daily soft drink sales of $300.

2. Between the test spot near the paddleboat dock and the spot that yielded $400 in hot dog sales, one generated $310 in soft drink sales and the other took in $210 in snack sales.

3. The location at the entrance to the zoo didn't yield $250 in snack sales, and the spot that generated $170 in snack sales (which was not the spot Harry set up at the busiest intersection in the park) didn't generate $350 in soft drink sales.

4. The location that garnered $370 in hot dog sales also brought in $330 in soft drink sales.

5. The paddleboat dock location generated more soft drink sales than the busiest intersection location but less than the spot by the zoo entrance. The test spot by the ball fields didn't garner $370 in hot dog sales or $250 in snack sales.

6. The dock location didn't produce $330 in soft drink sales; the spot that produced $310 in hot dog sales didn't also produce $350 in soft drink sales.

		Hot dog $				Snacks $				Soft drink $			
		$310	$340	$370	$400	$170	$190	$210	$250	$300	$310	$330	$350
Spot	ball fields												
	busiest road												
	boat dock												
	zoo entrance												
Soft drink $	$300												
	$310												
	$330												
	$350												
Snacks $	$170												
	$190												
	$210												
	$250												

№11 SPRUCING UP THE STREET

Home improvement-wise, it's been a busy spring this year down on the 1800 block of Shady Lane: four of the homeowners on the block upgraded by making substantial improvements to the outsides of their houses and on the grounds of their properties. See if you can figure out which homeowners did what to spiff up their homes and properties.

1. Between the house at 1807 Shady Lane and the house that got painted, one is a split-level and the other is fronted by a brand-new picket fence.

2. The new swimming pool (which is not behind the house that had its roof reshingled) was installed at one of the properties with an odd-numbered street address.

3. A circular driveway has been put in at 1807 Shady Lane, which is not where you find the rambler or where the roofing work was done.

4. The house at 1802 Shady Lane is not a cottage; the house at 1804 Shady Lane is not a two-story colonial, nor is it on the property with the nice new picket fence.

5. The owner of the house at 1815 Shady Lane did not enclose the screened-in side porch, nor is that house a rambler or colonial.

		Type of home				House				Grounds			
		cottage	rambler	split-level	2-story colonial	painting	enclosed porch	roof work	new windows	driveway	landscaping	picket fence	swimming pool
Address	1802 Shady Ln.												
	1804 Shady Ln.												
	1807 Shady Ln.												
	1815 Shady Ln.												
Grounds	driveway												
	landscaping												
	picket fence												
	swimming pool												
House	painting												
	enclosed porch												
	roof work												
	new windows												

№12 BUSY AFTERNOON AT THE AIRPORT

Metro International Airport was busy as usual this afternoon—39 planes (including a mix of prop planes, 2-engine jets, and 4-engine jets) were recorded as taking off between 3:00 and 5:00 p.m. See if you can deduce, from the info provided below, what the exact mix of departing planes was during each half-hour segment of this time period.

1. Between 4:00 and 4:30, there were fewer 4-engine jets taking off than during the following half hour but more than during the 3:00 to 3:30 period.

2. During none of the half-hour segments in which two additional 2-engine jets took off than in some other segment did three prop planes go airborne.

3. Between 3:30 and 4:00, five 2-engine jets, but not two prop planes nor three 4-engine jets, took off.

4. During the 3:00 to 3:30 segment, more prop planes departed than between 4:30 and 5:00, but fewer than between 3:30 and 4:00.

5. During the half-hour segment that two prop planes took off, neither four nor eight 2-engine jets did likewise; during the half-hour segment when three prop planes left, five 2-engine jets did not take off as well.

6. In neither half-hour period between 3:30 and 4:30 did one 4-engine jet depart; during the 4:00 to 4:30 period, neither six nor eight 2-engine jets took off.

		4-engine jets				2-engine jets				Prop planes			
		0	1	2	3	4	5	6	8	1	2	3	4
Time period	3:00 to 3:30												
	3:30 to 4:00												
	4:00 to 4:30												
	4:30 to 5:00												
Prop planes	1												
	2												
	3												
	4												
2-engine jets	4												
	5												
	6												
	8												

CHAPTER 4
MORE-CHALLENGING PUZZLES

CROSSWORD

ACROSS

1. Pick, with "for"
4. Fair shake, honest transaction
9. Mongolian desert
13. Rock's ___ Speedwagon
14. Sonata section
15. Ohio or Mississippi
16. Storage place on a ship
18. Month after deciembre
19. Prefix for "physics" or "logical"
20. Tau preceder
22. ___ Tin Tin
23. "___ be an honor!"
25. Mysterious Atlantic region
27. Legal advice
31. Rip
32. Swiss peaks
33. Political cartoonist called "our best recruiting sergeant" by Lincoln
36. Harvests
39. Outdoor gear brand
40. Figures that represent things or ideas, including four this puzzle uses
42. Winter bug
43. Coffee break snack
45. Far from ruddy
46. Halt
47. Government agent, briefly
49. Condensed readings
51. Secretive English tribunal of old
55. Italian monk
56. Fabrication
57. French Revolution leader
59. Gives off, as light
63. Expunge
65. Not flexible
67. German city close to Luxembourg
68. "Snowy" bird
69. Geologic time period
70. Filly's father
71. D shape
72. Encountered

DOWN

1. Killer whale
2. Pod contents
3. Civil wrong
4. 3 and 4, to 9 and 16
5. Homer's cry
6. Genesis name
7. Improvise
8. Skiers' hotel
9. Martini ingredient
10. Checking account problems
11. Soviet secret police chief
12. Area under Viet Minh control during the Vietnam War
15. Fruit squeezers
17. Big smiles
21. *The A-Team* actor
24. Declare untrue
26. Oil-rich fed.
27. Cash alternative
28. Butter alternative
29. Unsettled
30. Source of illumination
34. Govt. loan org. for mom-and-pop businesses
35. Tattled
37. Conspiracy
38. Has dinner
40. Speak haltingly
41. First name in New World exploration
44. Actress Thurman
46. Stitching lines
48. Pro hoops group
50. _____ route (shortest distance between, say, New York and Tokyo, taking you over Canada, northern Alaska, and Siberia)
51. Aspiring actresses
52. Wispy clouds
53. Iroquois enemies
54. Kitchen appliance
58. Kind of paper
60. Anagram for MITE
61. Goodyear product
62. "Shoo!"
64. Envision
66. Hawaiian garland

№15 FIGURATIVE THINKING

1	2	3		4	5	6	7	8			9	10	11	12
13				14						15				
16			17							18				
19					20			21			22			
			23		24		25			26				
27	28	29			30			31						
32					33		34	35		36			37	38
39				40					41			42		
43			44		45						46			
		47			48			49		50				
51	52				53	54		55						
56				57			58		59		60	61	62	
63			64		65			66						
67					68						69			
70					71						72			

1990S TRIVIA CHALLENGE

Who was appointed as the first female US secretary of state in 1997?

What was the highest-grossing movie at the box office in the 1990s?

ACROSS

1. Water balloon impact sound
6. Cloudless
11. French vineyard
14. Word preceding "potato," "stew," or "whiskey"
15. Door part
16. Emeritus: Abbr.
17. Cable channel popular with 1990s kids
19. Id ___ (that is)
20. Golfer's dream
21. End of a farm song's refrain
22. Run off together
24. Sheriff's badge, informally
27. Pittsburgh athlete
29. Send again, as a package
30. Cable network
31. Computer brand
32. "It's been _____ pleasure"
33. Denims
35. Foxy
36. Rock and Roll Hall of Fame thrash band
39. Chest protector
42. Indian currency unit
43. Most-wanted invitees
47. "Amazing Grace" ending
49. Humanities degs.
50. Spaces on a form left to be filled
51. Sachs' partner in finance
53. Dated name for a 2-wood
54. One of 50
55. Form of "to be"
56. *Walden* author's initials
57. On a roll
58. Venomous vipers
63. Unfold, poetically
64. Within walking distance
65. Plains mobile dwelling of yore
66. Danson or Nugent
67. Tacked on
68. Bird food

DOWN

1. "That's Life" singer
2. More costly
3. Driver's need
4. Inquire
5. Definite article
6. Hymn-singing group
7. Resort island near Venice
8. Charlotte-to-Raleigh dir.
9. "Give it ___!"
10. Actress Zellweger
11. Some Caribbean folks
12. Correct a typo, perhaps
13. Downright
18. Bound
23. Conducted
25. Fake
26. Person who installs ceramics
27. Fissile rock
28. *Beloved* author Morrison
30. Women's tennis great Monica
33. Where Akitas originated
34. La _____ opera house
37. Marching band instrument
38. "Oh, woe!"
39. VIP
40. Heavy hydrogen, e.g.
41. Overdue
44. Toned
45. Lost traction
46. African pests
48. DC summer hrs.
50. Chandler Harris's _____ Fox
52. Hajji's destination
53. Kennel club classification
55. Cathedral recess
59. Ancient
60. Herd of seals
61. Shaker ___, O.
62. Wide shoe spec.

№16 SOME ARE HEAVY

1	2	3	4	5	■	6	7	8	9	10	■	11	12	13
14					■	15					■	16		
17					18						■	19		
20			■	21			■	■	22	23				
24			25	26			■	27	28					
29					■	30			■	31				
32				■	33				34		■	35		
■	■	36		37						38	■	■	■
39	40	41	■	42				■	43		44	45	46
47		48	■	49			■	50					
51			52			■	53						
54				■	55				■	56			
57		■	58	59	60				61	62			
63			64			■	65						
66			67			■	68						

THINK ABOUT IT

The brain is a complex piece of circuitry that constantly is rewiring itself. When you learn something new, signals between neurons representing that learning are developed; as the learning is repeated, that neural connection becomes stronger. On the other hand, neural connections you don't use become weaker over time— giving credence to the slogan "use it or lose it."

ACROSS

1. Harmonize
5. Ayatollah's predecessor
9. Forest clearing
14. Creme-filled cookie
15. _____ Alto, Calif.
16. Broadcaster
17. Moniker for the skeptical *apostolo*
20. Buck's pride
21. Trounced
22. "There ____ tide . . ."
23. Name akin to Chas. or Wm.
24. Intense anger
25. Big Midwestern *citta*
29. Flying mammals
30. "____ y Plata" (Montana's motto)
31. Nick and Nora's pet
32. Mountain pool
34. Wine grape
36. A Manning
38. Kentucky Derby prize
41. Small bills
43. _____ II (razor brand)
45. Break bread
46. Playground retort
48. Member of a women's *religiosa* order
51. Catch a few Zs
52. Name of 12 popes
53. Jail, slangily
54. Essentially
56. Restrains
60. Theory that, within a business *organizzazione*, people tend to get promoted up to their level of incompetence
62. Mistake
63. Condo division
64. Boss Tweed skewerer
65. Itsy-bitsy
66. Russian news agency
67. Mardi _____

DOWN

1. Fountain order
2. "Pumping _____"
3. Neither masc. nor fem.
4. Mischievous creature of folklore
5. Well-thrown passes
6. Painter Holbein
7. HS math class
8. Frankfurter
9. Full range
10. Large branch
11. Indian Ocean arm
12. Wasteland
13. Wears down
18. Having a will
19. Satellite's path around the earth
23. Marketplaces or theater districts (named after a famous commercial area of Venice)
25. Absorb, with "up"
26. The Diamondbacks, on scoreboards
27. Area roughly 50 to 400 miles above the earth's surface
28. Arapaho foe
29. "My man!"
33. Antiquated
35. Musical Yoko
37. Like some verbs: Abbr.
39. Ring bearer, maybe
40. Amtrak stop: Abbr.
42. Vice President Agnew
44. Highlighting hues
46. All worked up
47. *Animal Farm*, e.g.
49. Yield
50. Baseball game segment
52. Fencer's defense
55. English prep school
56. Social reformer Jacob _____
57. Practice for a boxing match
58. Ingrid's *Casablanca* role
59. Brooklyn's NBA team
61. Genetic info carrier

№17 ITALICIZED ANSWERS

1	2	3	4		5	6	7	8		9	10	11	12	13
14					15					16				
17				18					19					
20							21							
			22				23					24		
25	26	27				28				29				
30				31					32	33				
34			35			36		37		38			39	40
		41			42		43		44			45		
46	47			48	49					50				
51				52				53						
54			55				56				57	58	59	
60						61								
62					63					64				
65					66					67				

DID YOU KNOW?

The word search puzzle, as we know it today, is said to have been created by Norman Gibat, the publisher of a free want-ad digest in Norman, Oklahoma, in 1968. Gibat inserted the puzzle in the digest as a way to hype his publication's distribution. The puzzle was an immediate hit and has remained popular ever since.

ACROSS

1. Unwanted email
5. IV amounts, briefly
8. Stages
14. Operatic solo
15. Org. for nonpaid athletes
16. Bewail, deplore
17. Hairstyling for the woman who wants to look good on the job?
19. Landlocked African country
20. Least difficult
22. Part of speech
23. Hawaiian strings
26. Large canvas covers for a fossil-containing natural asphalt deposit in suburban LA?
28. Housepainter's aid
30. Commits a faux pas
31. Deuce topper
32. Present occasion
34. Shade
37. Movie that reminisces about sunbathing during bygone vacation beach trips?
41. Comedienne Gasteyer
42. Young fellow, informally
43. Parentheses, e.g.
44. Bridge position
45. Taste
47. Agreement between two colleges to pool their teaching staffs?
52. Hankering
53. Explorer Erikson
54. Household chore
56. Recently
58. "Stop that!" . . . or a hint to solving 17-, 26-, 37-, and 47-Across
62. Candy units
63. Fruit drink brand
64. Approximately
65. Bourbon _____
66. Biblical verb suffix
67. Musical chairs goal

DOWN

1. Espied
2. Con's opposite
3. Put on TV
4. Manufacture
5. He preceded Augustus
6. West Indies native
7. Ancient Mesopotamian civilization
8. Ancient biographer of Augustus and other emperors
9. Witch
10. Some appliances
11. Mexican Mister
12. Eventually become
13. Musial and Getz
18. Ashen
21. Taken care of
23. The "U" in UHF
24. A Carpenter
25. Swelling
27. Certain surgeon's "patient"
29. Colorant
32. Bees collect this
33. Mork's planet
34. Mythical monster
35. "I give!"
36. Ruhr Valley city
38. Wharton degs.
39. Most thick and unruly, as a beard
40. Scottish cap
44. Wipe away
45. Stool pigeon
46. Lambs, in Latin
47. Falls heavily
48. Overhaul, as a ship
49. Petroleum-hauling ship
50. Swiss pharma giant
51. Indigenous Canadian
55. '60s muscle cars
57. Golf gadget
59. Bauxite, e.g.
60. ____ Today
61. Little one

№18 HIT DELETE

1	2	3	4	■	5	6	7	■	8	9	10	11	12	13
14				■	15			■	16					
17				18	■			■	19					
■	■		20					21	■	22				
23	24	25	■	26					■	27				
28			29			■		30			■	■	■	■
31				■		32	33				■	34	35	36
37				38	39					40				
41				42				■		43				
■	■		44				■	45	46					
47	48	49				50	51		■	52				
53				■	54					55	■	■	■	■
56				57		■	58				59	60	61	
62					■	63			■	64				
65					■	66			■	67				

THINK ABOUT IT

They say that variety is the spice of life. Whether that's so or not, what is true is that variety is good for your brain health. One recent study showed that adults who participate in a variety of activities are likely to have better cognitive abilities. Another study of older adults compared those who regularly pursue two or more physical and mental activities with those who only practice one and found that those who did multiple activities scored higher on tests measuring cognitive skills.

ACROSS

1. Pacific Islands country
6. Outpouring
11. Dynamite's kin
14. Squirrel's treat
15. Rockin' John
16. Brouhaha
17. Places for fowls with martial arts training?
19. Earlier
20. Dash
21. Solemn promise
22. "___ dias"
24. Tack room item
26. Floppy caps
28. Frenzy in Venice cheering a certain traveler's return in 1295?
32. Anagram for TOAST
35. Strong cleaners
36. Massage target
37. Broadcasting band, briefly
38. WWII zone
40. Cooking meas.
42. Golf clubhead part
43. Slew
45. European car name derived from the Latin for "listen"
47. City near Düsseldorf
49. Lounging jacket FDR wore when he got comfy in front of his potbellied stove?
52. End of a warning
53. Nebraska river
57. Egyptian amulet
59. Ante-
61. Barnyard bleats
62. Mason's trough
63. Does some courting after having just gotten a walk?
66. "Hail, Caesar!"
67. Chilean range
68. Digital promise of payment
69. Formerly part of HRH
70. Dublin-born poet and playwright
71. Commonly found substance, the chemical symbol for which, when sounded out, provides a hint for solving 17-, 28-, 49-, and 63-Across

DOWN

1. Scene-shooting units
2. City in Florida's horse country
3. *WarGames* org.
4. Doter, often
5. Hill dweller
6. Dry, as some Spanish wine
7. Farm lad
8. ___ Z
9. High rankers
10. Followed
11. Cuts across
12. Nixed, at NASA
13. Ark groupings
18. At any time
23. Sicilian landmark
25. Tardy
27. Ipecac, e.g.
29. Sun blockers
30. Brake part
31. As ____ On TV
32. Catch a wave
33. Laotian's neighbor
34. ATV driver
39. Coccyx
41. Ring out
44. Okla. until 1907
46. Like Garbo's eyes
48. Triathlete's need
50. St. Lawrence _____
51. Golf competition
54. Divination deck
55. Savory sense
56. "Poly" ender
57. Persian word for "king"
58. Inlet
60. "Happy little trees" painter Bob ____
64. Harem chamber
65. Sprinkling

№19 SWITCHEROO

1	2	3	4	5		6	7	8	9	10		11	12	13
14						15						16		
17					18							19		
20					21				22		23			
24				25			26	27						
		28			29							30	31	
32	33	34				35					36			
37				38	39			40		41		42		
43			44		45		46				47	48		
49				50				51						
		52						53				54	55	56
57	58					59	60				61			
62				63		64				65				
66				67					68					
69				70					71					

2000S TRIVIA CHALLENGE

In what year did Apple release its first iPhone?

Name the TV comedy show, structured as a mockumentary, that premiered in 2005 and ran until 2013.

ACROSS

1. Cries of discovery
5. Karaoke need, briefly
8. Big sister?
14. Home of the Rose Parade
16. Problem created by moisture
17. Person from Birmingham, say
18. Complete
19. Forwarding mail to an alternate address, say
21. Where a golf game begins
22. Big name in air-conditioning
23. Darjeeling and oolong
24. Helvetica or Calibri
25. Eddy around, as the wind
27. Valley _____
28. Overlook
32. Fireplace shelf
33. Late-night's Conan
34. Last but two, in a series
37. Lipitor, for one
38. "Balderdash!"
39. Lost traction
40. Multiroom hotel accommodation
41. Church council
43. Catalan surrealist
44. Cracker topper
45. Accustom: Var.
50. Catchall abbr.
51. Sterna
53. Devil, in Durango
55. With these, we sometimes see what's on the bottom
56. Pants measurement
57. Having the power to radiate . . . or possibly what one could call a text
58. Insurance sellers
59. Cap. Hill VIP
60. Hebrew for "delight"

DOWN

1. Not together
2. More healthy and vigorous
3. Carne _____ (burrito filling)
4. Polio vaccine developer
5. Hand raiser's insistent cry
6. Lack of movement
7. Collection of stories published around 1400 that has become a literary classic (with "The")
8. Words of agreement
9. Crosby
10. Lunch counter order, for short
11. Newspaper opinion piece
12. Area of Africa famed, among other things, for its lion population
13. Made, as a deal, even more attractive
15. Starts of some pranks
20. Suffix with president, proverb, or potent
24. The IRS has plenty of these
26. "Say _____"
27. Most Wanted List org.
28. Array of organizations like broadcasters and newspapers that reach large audiences
29. Figuring out instinctively
30. Feature of a two-story house
31. Brief brawl
33. Palindromic man's name
35. Chart type
36. _____ Dove (McMurtry novel)
41. Motor oil letters
42. Bankruptcy listings
44. High school social events
46. Clamor
47. Overturned
48. His is the third story in 7-Down
49. German industrial hub
51. Horn sound
52. Romulus or Remus
54. Stiller or Kingsley

№20 NO THEME, BUT CHALLENGING

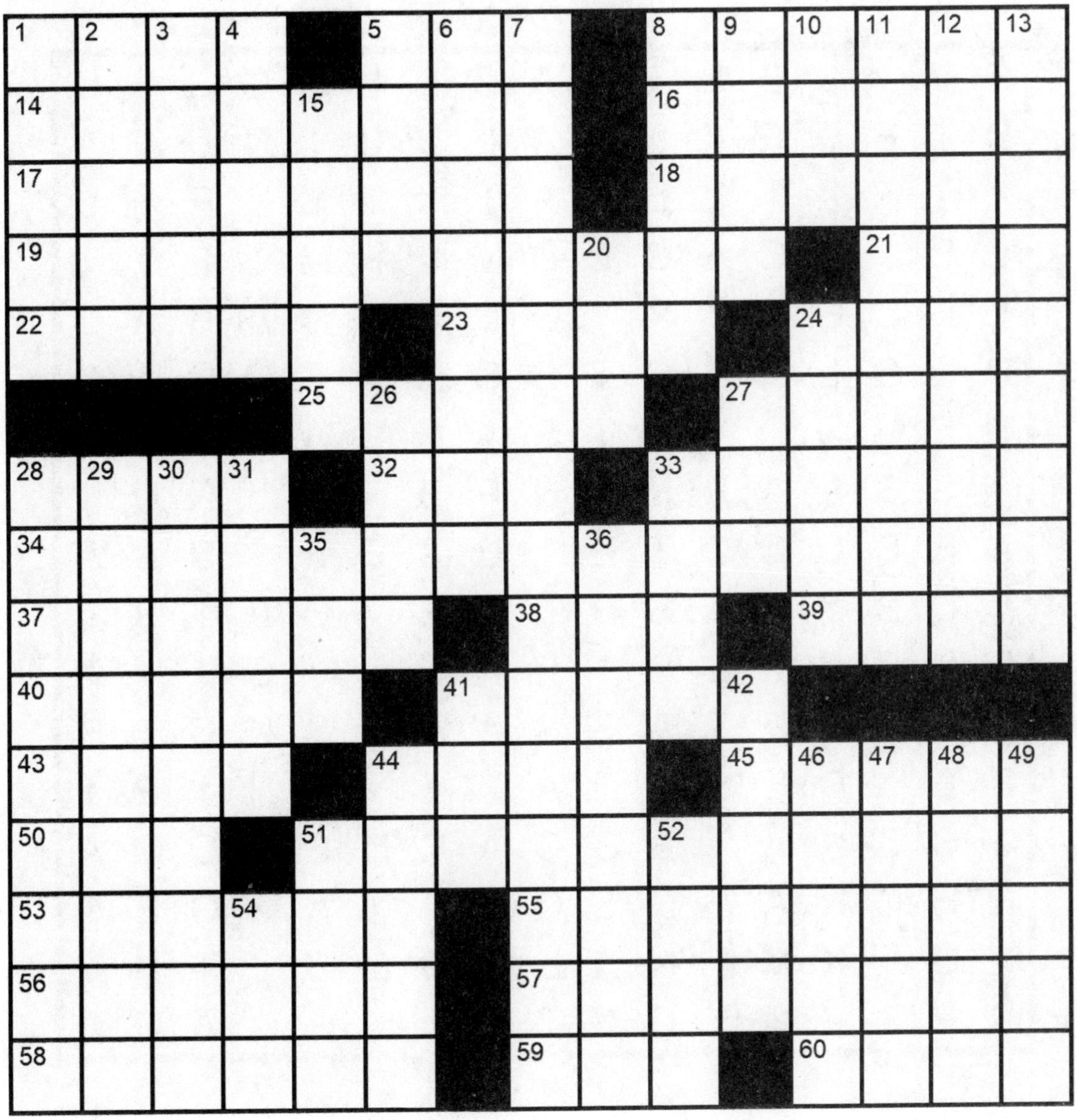

THINK ABOUT IT

Nutrition experts advise that all foods are not created equal when it comes to maintaining and improving brain health. Among the foods that top the brain-healthy list because of all the important micronutrients they contain are leafy greens; fatty fish like salmon, cod, and tuna; berries; and walnuts.

№15 HOW TO GET FROM HERE TO THERE

```
P M I L B G T R A C F L O G S S D
D T E N E A L R A L U C I N U F A
Y I R L I L L I A I X T S B R T U
L E N E C A C L D M L F M T F Y T
L E L G T Y R Y O E J A O A B A O
R E O L H P C T C O R R Z O O W G
O E M N O Y O I S I N C W B A B E
T S S A A R K C N P B R D L R U N
A R B C C C T E I U Z E J I D S A
V O B Y A A S H L L E V C A T S L
E H C P O L S I P P E O J S I I P
L L T B E T A S S W A H S K C I R
E E W D E S E T A X I Y S H I P I
J O S K A T E B O A R D E P O M A
R H C R A F D L Q R D Y A W G E S
V O A K M F N R E T O O C S T H V
R P S L U Y C F T F I L R I A H C
```

AIRPLANE	FUNICULAR	RICKSHAW	SPEEDBOAT
AUTO	GLIDER	ROCKET SHIP	SUBMARINE
BICYCLE	GOLF CART	ROWBOAT	SUBWAY
BLIMP	HELICOPTER	SAILBOAT	SURFBOARD
CAMEL	HORSE	SCOOTER	TAXI
CANOE	hot-air BALLOON	SEGWAY	TRAIN
CHAIRLIFT	HOVERCRAFT	SHIP	TRAM
DINGHY	JETPACK	SKATEBOARD	TROLLEY
ELEVATOR	MOPED	SKATES	UNICYCLE
ESCALATOR	MOTORCYCLE	SKIS	
FERRY	PARASAIL	SLED	

№16 YUMMY DESSERTS

```
M N H M F A O M E A D N U S B W B
E A O A O C B I S M O R E S A A U
R T C E L U A L E D U R T S K H S
F R J A L V S K E S E D T E L M I
U A E E R O A S E M B L D E A R M
A T L K U O P H E A H A F E V M A
G E L A T O N A B C L C R F A U R
N B O C T T O K N A U C A D U C I
I P A E R U A E S G E S E E A O T
D A F S I R I K A C W L T N P C S
D R L E F N A T I F E F N A U I I
U F A E L O R E T I F O R P R T E
P A N H E V E H N O L O C U O D K
E I P C I E Z E J I C A G R I M O
A T I N A R G K Z G K S T A I T O
X O W E U G N I R E M E I A T T C
S O R R U H C T E N G I E B T O X
```

AFFOGATO	CUPCAKE	MADELEINE	SOUFFLE
BABKA	CUSTARD	MERINGUE	STRUDEL
BAKED ALASKA	FLAN	MILKSHAKE	SUNDAE
BAKLAVA	FRUIT	MOUSSE	TART
BEIGNET	GAUFRE	NAPOLEON	TIRAMISU
BISCOTTI	GELATO	PARFAIT	TORTE
CAKE	GRANITA	PEACH MELBA	TRIFLE
CANNOLI	HALVAH	PIE	TURNOVER
CHEESECAKE	ICE CREAM	PROFITEROLE	
CHURROS	JELL-O	PUDDING	
COOKIES	MACARON	S'MORES	

№17 OUR FEATHERED FRIENDS

```
C K R O D N O C O K V F L S S
H S R F Q G R O B I N W T P I
I C W A N O R E H W O I A L B
C C N A L B B X T I L R S C I
K U R I L A L B A T R O S S L
E E N A F L N E L O I R O L B
N G O E N D O I W C D B U K G
Z R C T H E R W D X U G F P A
P E L I C A N W Y R A C A U T
Z T A K I G W A D E A R K W E
N H F L C L J K S G R C M O C
E R E K C E P D O O W P D R O
V U L T U R E U T O P O S C V
A S Z L Y B R C N S V L I O A
R H B S T O R K B E K I R H S
```

ALBATROSS	CUCKOO	KIWI	SHRIKE
AUK	DOVE	LARK	SPARROW
AVOCET	DUCK	ORIOLE	STILT
BALD EAGLE	EGRET	OSPREY	STORK
BITTERN	FALCON	OWL	SWALLOW
BLUE JAY	FINCH	PARROT	THRUSH
CARDINAL	GOOSE	PELICAN	VULTURE
CHICKEN	HAWK	RAIL	WOODPECKER
CONDOR	HERON	RAVEN	
CRANE	IBIS	ROBIN	
CROW	KITE	SEAGULL	

№18 FAMOUS NOVELISTS

```
F  T  D  N  A  R  I  X  V  O  M  I  S  A  J  P  A
O  A  R  E  K  L  A  W  S  T  Z  V  F  U  Z  E  L
G  G  U  W  F  D  V  C  O  T  E  H  J  S  I  T  C
D  K  U  L  A  O  D  L  A  R  E  G  Z  T  I  F  O
P  U  S  H  K  I  N  D  N  M  N  V  S  E  G  A  T
X  L  M  O  R  N  J  E  I  W  U  I  E  N  T  Y  T
S  E  B  A  I  E  E  N  O  C  R  S  I  N  K  X  U
C  A  E  A  S  I  G  R  B  H  K  L  Q  S  S  G  G
N  V  W  M  D  W  B  N  C  Z  P  E  V  L  N  O  E
L  T  P  H  A  W  E  Z  I  I  G  E  N  I  X  A  N
L  R  S  Y  I  H  C  T  K  L  O  N  K  S  O  Y  N
O  U  J  L  E  A  S  Z  N  T  A  G  I  B  R  O  O
R  H  D  M  O  R  R  I  S  O  N  S  E  M  W  T  V
R  E  H  W  A  T  T  O  R  T  R  C  N  O  E  S  Y
A  A  T  W  O  O  D  R  Q  G  Y  B  O  Z  L  L  L
C  J  N  O  D  N  O  L  A  O  Y  L  W  U  L  O  F
Y  E  L  L  E  H  S  V  J  S  F  E  L  I  O  T  D
```

ALCOTT, louisa may

ASIMOV, isaac

ATWOOD, margaret

AUSTEN, jane

BRONTE, charlotte

BROWN, dan

CAMUS, albert

CARROLL, lewis

CHRISTIE, agatha

DICKENS, charles

DOSTOEVSKY, fyodor

DUMAS, alexandre

ELIOT, george

FAULKNER, william

FITZGERALD, f. scott

FLEMING, ian

GRISHAM, john

HEMINGWAY, ernest

HUGO, victor

JOYCE, james

KAFKA, franz

KING, stephen

KIPLING, rudyard

LEE, harper

LONDON, jack

MORRISON, toni

NABOKOV, vladimir

ORWELL, george

PUSHKIN, alexander

RAND, ayn

RUSHDIE, salman

SALINGER, j. d.

SARTRE, jean-paul

SHELLEY, mary

STEVENSON, robert
   louis

TOLSTOY, leo

TWAIN, mark

VERNE, jules

VONNEGUT, kurt

WALKER, alice

WHARTON, edith

WILDE, oscar

WOOLF, virginia

```
Q D W P N T C E W E L T T E K O S
U X Q S B I X L E S D S L J P J Y
P C H I S E L D L Y P K R A V W G
H A I R N A U O R A R S N W S Z D
Q Q W B G G Q E O I V A U O D U A I
N P B U M B X D Y V N L G N L G B
S U R H P C B P U V L B V U T J Q
Y F T Z S W O B L E P E X C A A G
U C U M L M S X Y K I E P O U V D
L I N T E L I M Y L G U T J Q Q P
I R G N E G M N B G K S D U Y S V
A L W E I N X A B B E Z I P P E R
C W H G J E G Z R T X N J M A P O
A W H L R B V J S B C D N G L A L
H H U X R U E E Q E L P O L L A G
T Y E L C E I H K Q B E P A O A X
I S Q C L R E V I H S I X Q R Z M
```

AUGURY	HUBRIS	OXYGEN	VIOLIN
BASALT	ITHACA	PALLOR	WHEELS
CHISEL	JOCUND	QUINCE	XERXES
DOODLE	KETTLE	REUBEN	YELLOW
ELBOWS	LINTEL	SHIVER	ZIPPER
FRUGAL	MARBLE	TSETSE	
GALLOP	NUTMEG	UNVEIL	

№20 MISSING VOWELS

The puzzle grid contains no vowels, only circles where the vowels should be. Your challenge is to fill in the vowels as you locate the key words. Every circle will be filled when the puzzle is completely solved.

ANTHEM	FREER	NEGLECT	STOVE
BLIP	FUSION	PERT	SUPPRESS
BRIEF	GORGE	PILOT	TICKET
BUTTON	ICING	QUOTE	TOPPER
CATTLE	LAVA	REJOIN	TRIANGLE
ELEVATOR	LEVER	ROBOT	TROOPER
ERRAND	MARKET	SECTOR	WIDE
EXIST	MITTENS	SHAMPOO	WIDOW
FLAVOR	NATTER	SKIMPED	WILLOW

№14 DON'T BE COWED

BP EXFD GKIPDEKS, XDR AZLIXEP, XDR AZDOFRPDAP

_____

NH PXAS PMUPIFPDAP FD BSFAS BP IPXCCH GKZU KZ

_____

CZZQ OPXI FD KSP OXAP... BP VLGK RZ KSXK BSFAS

_____

BP KSFDQ BP AXDDZK RZ.

_____

—PCPXDZI IZZGPJPCK

_____

HINT (SEE PAGE 124): 18

№15 FORWARD-LOOKING IDEAL

PCW NQQWIPFKX PCNP "NBB OWX NIW EIWNPWR

_____

WMLNB" HNQ KT XK JINEPFENB LQW FX WTTWEPFXA

_____

KLI QWJNINPFKX TIKO AIWNP UIFPNFX NXR FP HNQ

_____

JBNEWR FX PCW RWEBNINPFKX XKP TKI PCNP, ULP TKI

_____

TLPLIW LQW.

_____

—NUINCNO BFXEKBX

_____

HINT (SEE PAGE 124): 16

№16 THE AUTHOR'S PRODUCT

PLPFH FPVQPF MXDQU WXIUPAM. BWP JFXBPF'U JNFG

_____

XU IPFPAH V GXDQ NM NCBXKVA XDUBFZIPDB BWVB

_____

IVGPU XB CNUUXTAP MNF BWP FPVQPF BN QXUKPFD

_____

JWVB, JXBWNZB BWXU TNNG, WP JNZAQ CPFWVCU

_____

DPLPF WVLP UPPD XD WXIUPAM.

_____

—IVFKPA CFNZUB

_____

HINT (SEE PAGE 124): 22

№17 THE MAGIC OF THE WOODS

VK VB XTK BT AFSO QTI VKB DJPFKW KOPK KOJ QTIJBK

_____

APZJB P SEPVA FHTX HJTHEJ'B OJPIKB, PB QTI KOPK

_____

BFDKEJ BTAJKOVXR, KOPK CFPEVKW TQ PVI, KOPK

_____

JAPXPKVTX QITA TEU KIJJB, KOPK BT GTXUJIQFEEW

_____

SOPXRJB PXU IJXJGB P GJPIW BHVIVK.

_____

—ITDJIK ETFVB BKJMJXBTX

_____

HINT (SEE PAGE 124): 4

№18 MORE ISN'T ALWAYS BETTER

KV MOQ PWXXQVM EWPNKNI, WR WM WV WJ

_____

UWVBNUQN, WV JBM KV GVQRGE KV K VTKEE PGM

_____

DQEE–KNNKJXQU BJQ, VB IBG TKI KYYGTGEKMQ K LKVM

_____

KTBGJM BR SJBDEQUXQ PGM WM DWEE PQ BR RKN

_____

EQVV LKEGQ MOKJ K TGYO VTKEEQN KTBGJM WR IBG

_____

OKLQ JBM MOBGXOM WM BLQN RBN IBGNVQER.

_____

—KNMOGN VYOBZQJOKGQN

_____

HINT (SEE PAGE 124): 1

№19 MERCY, THE HIGHEST VIRTUE

API MB VCI AWBIPV IC IJCBP LJC IJWVR LP CMYJI IC

_____

NP XVYUG LWIJ CMU PVPDWPB, XVO LJC NPAWPHP

_____

IJWB IC NP YUPXI XVO DXVAG. VCIJWVY WB BC

_____

EUXWBPLCUIJG, VCIJWVY BC TAPXUAG BJCLB X YUPXI

_____

XVO VCNAP BCMA, XB TAPDPVTG XVO UPXOWVPBB IC

_____

QCUYWHP.

_____

—TWTPUC

_____

HINT (SEE PAGE 124): 35

SUDOKU №16

							9	6
			3	2		7		
	5	8			1			
		1		6				
6		3				2		4
			1			8		
			7			9	2	
		5		8	4			
3	8							

SUDOKU №17

2				3	1		8	
1					5		3	
			4	6				
						2	5	
		2	3		8	7		
	7	4						
			5	6				
	9		2					7
	5		9	4				3

SUDOKU №18

9	7		8			4		
						9	2	1
	2		5					8
				3				4
			4		8			
5				1				
2					7		5	
7	3	6						
		4			6		7	2

SUDOKU №19

								9
5			6		9	1		
	7	2					8	
	4	5	3					
1								7
					8	9	4	
	5					8	3	
		9	5		7			6
4								

SUDOKU №20

	8			3				5
					6		1	
		5	4			7	2	
		3	1		8			
8				7				1
			9		5	2		
	1	7			4	5		
	2		5					
6				1			4	

SUDOKU №21

			7	8	6	5		
3	6		9					
		8				7		
8			3				9	2
1	3				2			8
		2				4		
					3		1	6
		3	5	4	1			

CALCUDOKU

CALCUDOKU №14

1-		10+	9+		72×
7+					
4	18×	8+		4×	6+
15×		9+			
	1		30×		2
2-		5 :		1-	

CALCUDOKU №15

8+	0-		2-	4+	
		3+		24×	9+
11+					
	13+		60×		
4×				3 :	
	11+		2-		3

CALCUDOKU №16

10+		5+		1-	
	30×	5+	13+		2 :
7+				3-	
	60×		5+		10+
6 :				3-	
	20×				3

CALCUDOKU №17

8+		8+		4-	2 :
4×	8+		17+		
		7+			3-
14+				4 :	
		2-			1-
5-		5		3	

CALCUDOKU №18

9+	2×		1-		10+
	9+			6×	
	24×		10×		8+
12×	2 :			4×	
		14+			2×
7+			2-		

CALCUDOKU №19

6+			9+		30×
30×	24×		2-		
	80×		5-		2-
		14+	6×		
	5-			30×	
3		1-			

FUTOSHIKI

FUTOSHIKI №14

FUTOSHIKI №15

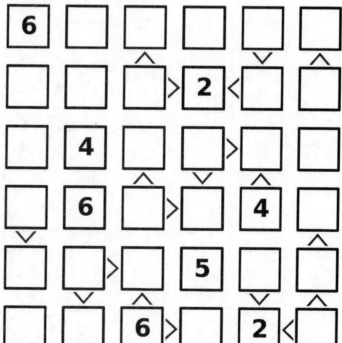

FUTOSHIKI №16

		1 <		6 >	
	v			v	
		>			4
	^				
		<	>		
		v			
	3				
	^		^	^	
<	>	>	2	5	
					^
		<	<	3 <		

FUTOSHIKI №17

>		4	5 <		
			v		^
>	4			3 <	
v					v
<	6				3
			^	^	
>	<				
v					
1					
^				v	
	>		>	4	1

FUTOSHIKI №18

3 < □	□	□ < □	7	□
6	□	□	5	1	2
□	□	□	□	5 < □	□
□	7	□ < 6	□	□	3
□	□	4	□	□ < □ < □
□	□	3 < □	□	1
□	□	□ < □ > □	□	2	□

DID YOU KNOW?

The Futoshiki puzzle was developed in 2001 in Japan, where it quickly became popular. Interest in the puzzle spread to Great Britain later in the 2000s, and it now is carried by several major British newspapers. The name is Japanese for "not equal."

№13 SATURDAY'S FARMERS MARKET

It's late on a summer Saturday afternoon, and the five vendors who provide produce for Middletown's Farmers Market are packing up and preparing to head back to their farms. Looking over their shoulders as they compare notes on what was sold today, you will see that, not unexpectedly, tomatoes and ears of corn were the best sellers. Based on the data below (all volumes are rounded to the nearest 10), see if you can figure out each vendor's volume of tomato and corn sales and who sold the most of each product. And, by the way, all five have their own little niche product that they also sell. So, see if you can also couple each niche product with a vendor.

1. The vendors include Doug's Delicious, the vendor who also sells country ham and biscuits on the side, the vendor who sold the most tomatoes today, and the vendor who sold 420 ears of corn.

2. Neither the vendor who sold 440 ears of corn nor the one who sold the most corn moved more than 160 pounds of tomatoes.

3. Hank's Produce sold more tomatoes today than the vendor who also offered farmstead cheese to customers (who wasn't the one who sold 400 ears of corn).

4. Farmer John B. markets potpourri along with his veggies; Fresh-from-the-Farm doesn't offer jars of apple butter along with its produce, and it did not sell 400 or 500 ears of corn nor 130 or 170 pounds of tomatoes.

5. Julie & Joe's doesn't bring honey or the ham/biscuit combo to the market to sell, nor did that vendor move 420 ears of corn today.

6. Hank is not the purveyor of ham and biscuits either, but he did sell 180 pounds of tomatoes; Farmer John didn't sell 400 ears of corn.

7. Doug doesn't sell apple butter or honey at the market and didn't sell 130 pounds of tomatoes today.

		Niche item					Tomatoes					Corn				
		apple butter	farm cheese	ham/biscuit	honey	potpourri	130 lbs.	160 lbs.	170 lbs.	180 lbs.	200 lbs.	340 ears	400 ears	420 ears	440 ears	500 ears
Vendor	Doug's Delicious															
	Farmer John B.															
	Fresh-Farm															
	Hank's Produce															
	Julie & Joe's															
Corn	340 ears															
	400 ears															
	420 ears															
	440 ears															
	500 ears															
Tomatoes	130 lbs.															
	160 lbs.															
	170 lbs.															
	180 lbs.															
	200 lbs.															

DID YOU KNOW?

Charles Dodgson—more familiarly known by his pen name Lewis Carroll, author of *Alice's Adventures in Wonderland*—is credited with creating the first narrative logic puzzle. In a book he published in 1886, *The Game of Logic,* he used a narrative game to demonstrate the use of logic to solve problems. However, he didn't employ a logic puzzle grid in connection with the game; those didn't make an appearance until well into the 20th century.

№14 PACIFIC ISLAND NATIONS

While the Pacific Ocean is vast, it is not empty. It is filled with many, many relatively small populated islands. The people in some island groups have formed nations, including the five included in this puzzle: Fiji, Palau, Samoa, Solomon Islands, and Tonga. Your challenge is to take the limited information provided below and deduce, for each country, the number of islands that make up the nation and the name and size of its largest island. BTW: none of the information here is made up; these are the real facts about each country.

1. Tonga's largest island is Tongatapu, which doesn't rank first or second among the five countries' biggest islands in size.

2. Palau has more islands than Fiji but less than the Solomon Islands.

3. The 659-square-mile "biggest island" is not Guadalcanal or part of Fiji. Tonga's "big island" is not the 143-square-mile one.

4. Babeldaob is not 2,047 square miles in size and is smaller than Savai'i, which is smaller than Guadalcanal (which doesn't measure 4,026 square miles.) Tongatapu is not 659 square miles in size.

5. Vita Levu is not in the Solomon Islands or Samoa or in the country made up of 340 islands.

6. Fiji is made up of 333 islands, while the Solomon Islands don't number 169.

7. Palau's "big island" is not 659 square miles in size. Savai'i is not part of a country that is made up of 340 or 992 islands. Neither Samoa nor Tonga claims 992 islands either.

8. Neither Samoa nor Palau is made up of 169 islands, nor can those two countries claim a "big island" that is 2,047 square miles in size.

	No. of islands					Largest island					Size of island				
	9	169	333	340	992	Babeldaob	Guadalcanal	Savai'i	Tongatapu	Vita Levu	101 sq. mi.	143 sq. mi.	659 sq. mi.	2,047 sq. mi.	4,026 sq. mi.
Nation Fiji															
Palau															
Samoa															
Solomon Islands															
Tonga															
Size of island 101 sq. mi.															
143 sq. mi.															
659 sq. mi.															
2,047 sq. mi.															
4,026 sq. mi.															
Largest island Babeldaob															
Guadalcanal															
Savai'i															
Tongatapu															
Vita Levu															

2010S TRIVIA CHALLENGE

Where were the 2012 Summer Olympic Games held?

Name the actor who won the 2013 Best Actor Academy Award for his portrayal of Lincoln in the movie of the same name.

№ 15 ICE CREAM SHOPS

Ike is the owner of YummyServ, a chain of ice cream shops in his hometown that has grown over the years so that now Ike has five locations. See if you can figure out, based on the clues below, in what order the five shops were opened, where each is located, its manager's name, and how many ice cream cones it sells each week (all data on cone sales are rounded to the nearest 50).

1. The YummyServ at the airport was opened before the one on the waterfront near the tourist traffic but after the store that Mike manages.

2. Between the third store Ike opened and the one headed by Mark, one is downtown and the other averages 1,850 ice cream cone sales a week.

3. Neither Ike's second shop (which is not run by Mack) nor the fourth shop sells precisely 100 more ice cream cones per week than another YummyServ store.

4. The third store Ike started sells fewer ice cream cones than the fifth but more than the first.

5. Neither the YummyServ location managed by Margo nor the one managed by Mike runs No. 1 or 2 in ice cream cone sales.

6. Melissa operates the third store Ike founded, but it doesn't generate 1,700 cone sales per week, and the store led by Mack does not sell the most cones per week.

7. The operation near the university is not Ike's first shop, and neither the one at the mall nor the one down at the waterfront is his third.

8. The shop averaging 1,650 cone sales per week is not Ike's original shop, the fourth one he opened, or the downtown shop; the shop averaging 1,800 cone sales per week is the one in which either Margo or Mark is managing things.

		Location					Manager					Cones served				
		airport	downtown	shopping mall	near school	waterfront	Margo	Mark	Mack	Melissa	Mike	1,650	1,700	1,800	1,850	1,900
Order opened	first															
	second															
	third															
	fourth															
	fifth															
Cones served	1,650															
	1,700															
	1,800															
	1,850															
	1,900															
Manager	Margo															
	Mark															
	Mack															
	Melissa															
	Mike															

THINK ABOUT IT

Engaging in physical exercise is a real "twofer": you get the benefit of improving your physical health and, as you do so, you are enhancing your cognitive fitness as well. Research studies show that exercise, especially aerobic exercise, leads to improved brain function. Even light-intensity physical activity will benefit your brain health.

№16 CONTAINER SHIPS

It's going to be a busy day for the harbor pilots at the Port of West Coast City today. Five large container ships, which have unloaded their inbound shipping containers, have taken on loads of containers in preparation for leaving port today, one departing every two hours starting at 9 AM. See if you can deduce, based on the information set out below, which ship is leaving when and how many containers each ship brought into port and will be leaving with.

1. MV PRECISION is not heading out to sea at 9 AM today; the MV MARLAK is leaving just before the MV ISAAC J. Neither MV PRECISION nor the container ship leaving port at 11 AM carried 7,900 shipping containers into port or is taking that number out of port.

2. The number of shipping containers that MV VICEROY is leaving with measures in the even hundreds, but not so the number of containers it brought in to be unloaded. The ship leaving at 11 AM will not have 7,400 containers on board, and the ship leaving at 5 PM won't be carrying 8,110 containers.

3. Between MV MARYSUE and the ship departing at 1 PM, one is leaving with 8,110 containers, and the other offloaded 6,550 containers on arrival.

4. MV MARLAK carried fewer containers than MV MARYSUE into port but more than did the MV ISAAC J (which is not carrying the largest load of containers out of port of the five leaving today).

5. MV ISAAC J sets sail at 5 PM today but won't be carrying the smallest or second-smallest outbound load of containers of the five; MV PRECISION does not set sail at 11 AM, nor is its cargo the largest number of containers moving in or out of port.

6. MV VICEROY is shipping more containers out of port than MV PRECISION but less than MV MARLAK or MV MARYSUE, which is shipping fewer containers than the MARLAK.

7. Neither MV MARYSUE nor MV VICEROY brought 6,830 containers into port; MV VICEROY also didn't bring in 8,130 containers, and MV ISAAC J didn't bring in 7,900 containers.

		Depart time					Inbound					Outbound				
		9:00 AM	11:00 AM	1:00 PM	3:00 PM	5:00 PM	6,550 cont.	6,830 cont.	7,250 cont.	7,900 cont.	8,130 cont.	5,900 cont.	7,400 cont.	7,900 cont.	8,110 cont.	8,750 cont.
Ship	MV ISAAC J															
	MV MARLAK															
	MV MARYSUE															
	MV PRECISION															
	MV VICEROY															
Outbound	5,900 cont.										
	7,400 cont.										
	7,900 cont.										
	8,110 cont.										
	8,750 cont.										
Inbound	6,550 cont.					
	6,830 cont.					
	7,250 cont.					
	7,900 cont.					
	8,130 cont.					

DID YOU KNOW?

Sudoku, Calcudoku, and Futoshiki all make use of what is called a Latin square, that is, a grid consisting of symbols or digits equal in number to the size of the grid (e.g., if the grid is 5x5, it is filled with iterations of the numbers 1 through 5) arranged so that each symbol or digit is used just once in each row and column. It got the moniker "Latin square" because Leonhard Euler, the 18th-century mathematician who developed the math theory behind this unusual sort of grid, used Latin characters, not numbers, in his grids.

№17 RANKING THE BEST BEACHES

A travel magazine has come out with a feature article ranking the five best beaches in the South that front the Atlantic Ocean. The article focuses on each beach's best natural feature and the top human touch that enhances the beach's standing. Using the statements below, each capturing some snippets of information from the article, see if you can piece together a thumbnail description of the features that make each beach special and how it ranked.

1. Included in the article's list of five best beaches are: Boka Beach, the beach ranked No. 5, a beach renowned for its sugary-looking white sand, a beach that is a state park, and Southwinds Beach.

2. Neither the No. 1- nor No. 2-ranked beach is known for its elaborate boardwalk or the many summer rental beach houses dotting its dunes; Johnsonville Beach does not have a long pier with a high-rated restaurant on it.

3. Orange Coast Beach is third ranked of the five, yet it is not known for its white sand nor having first-class purveyors of shore gear like surfboards, parasails, and snorkeling equipment.

4. The beach ranked No. 2 isn't the one with the gear-provisioning shops or the one known for its gentle waves and clear, shallow water.

5. Neither Saturn Beach nor the beach that has explorable coral reefs just offshore is ranked No. 5; nor is Saturn Beach known for the array of shore gear available there.

6. Boka Beach is not ranked in the article as high as Saturn Beach; Johnsonville Beach is not recognized for its beach houses or the exceptional width of the beach itself.

7. The beach that is a state park is known for its big waves, while the beach ranked No. 1 is not known for its width.

	Ranking					Natural feature					Added feature				
	5	4	3	2	1	snorkeling reefs	shallow water	great waves	white sand	wide beach	boardwalk	equipment	pier/restaurant	beach houses	state park
Beach Boka															
Johnsonville															
Orange Coast															
Saturn															
Southwinds															
Added feature boardwalk															
equipment															
pier/restaurant															
beach houses															
state park															
Natural feature snorkeling reefs															
shallow water															
great waves															
white sand															
wide beach															

THINK ABOUT IT

It's not all downhill for the aging brain. As we get older, the brain's physical make-up changes in a way that strengthens connections between distant brain areas. This enhances our ability to detect relationships among multiple sources of information, which in turn allows us to get a better sense of the "big picture" on matters of concern or interest to us.

№18 EXCITING FINISH AT THE SPEEDWAY

It was a great day for auto racing fans today with the running of the Southern Challenge 400. People at the speedway and watching on TV saw the first five finishers battle back and forth for the lead in the final laps, with all five crossing the finish line within 10 seconds of one another. Based on the fragmentary reports set out below, can you tell the order of finish for these five driving aces and which one claimed the checkered flag?

1. The five top finishers were Steve Stocker, Phil Fleet, the driver of car No. 27, the driver sponsored by Acme Auto Parts, and the fifth-place finisher.

2. The driver of car No. 50, who is not Phil Fleet, came in second.

3. Between Doug Draftin and the racer in car No. 9, one is sponsored by A+ Engine Additives and the other came in fourth.

4. Stu Speedster finished behind Phil Fleet but ahead of Pete Piston, and Doug Draftin didn't come in the last of the top five finishers.

5. Car No. 73 did not come in first or fourth, and the car sponsored by Chewy Candy Bar didn't place fourth either.

6. Neither car No. 16 nor the car sponsored by Fizzy Cola came in fifth among this elite group of drivers.

7. Fizzy Cola sponsored car No. 50, but neither Chewy nor Marvel Bread is Pete Piston's sponsor.

	Car number					Sponsor					Finish				
	9	16	27	50	73	Chewy Candy	A+ Engine Add.	Fizzy Cola	Marvel Bread	Acme Auto Parts	first	second	third	fourth	fifth
Racer Steve Stocker															
Phil Fleet															
Doug Draftin															
Pete Piston															
Stu Speedster															
Finish first															
second															
third															
fourth															
fifth															
Sponsor Chewy Candy															
A+ Engine Add.															
Fizzy Cola															
Marvel Bread															
Acme Auto Parts															

2020S TRIVIA CHALLENGE

What movie was No. 1 in domestic US box office receipts in 2021?

What was named the fastest-growing sport in the US in both 2021 and 2022?

SOLUTIONS

CRYPTOGRAM HINTS
(coded letter + real letter)

1	W = I	14	X = C	27	B = N
2	E = Y	15	X = C	28	W = T
3	G = O	16	C = H	29	A = N
4	K = T	17	Y = G	30	J = O
5	F = A	18	P = E	31	C = O
6	G = O	19	B = R	32	D = S
7	B = T	20	K = O	33	C = N
8	J = E	21	V = I	34	B = N
9	G = O	22	P = E	35	P = E
10	D = I	23	C = N	36	T = F
11	M = T	24	P = T	37	V = I
12	J = R	25	P = I	38	E = T
13	K = M	26	N = L	39	X = N

CHAPTER 1 SOLUTIONS

CROSSWORD 1

D	I	E	T	S		S	A	F	E		S	P	I	N
E	N	N	U	I		P	L	A	N		A	I	D	E
W	H	A	T	C	H	A	M	A	C	A	L	L	I	T
L	A	B	S			I	T	S		O	R	S	O	
A	L	L		Y	D	S		C	R	E	A	T	O	R
P	E	E	R	E	D		T	R	E	S		I	R	E
		A	T	E	A	S	E			S	N	O	B	
	T	H	I	N	G	A	M	A	J	I	G			
E	Y	E	S			A	R	E	N	A	S			
R	O	M		H	A	T	S		A	R	I	S	E	S
S	U	P	R	E	M	E		A	L	S		I	L	L
		E	I	R	E		C	I	O		I	N	D	O
I	N	S	P	E	C	T	O	R	G	A	D	G	E	T
R	O	T	E		H	A	L	E		F	L	E	S	H
A	S	S	N		E	R	A	S		T	E	S	T	S

WORD SEARCH 1

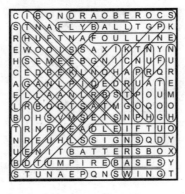

CRYPTOGRAM 1

LET'S BE PRACTICAL

Which painting in the National Gallery would I save if there was a fire? The one nearest the door of course.

—George Bernard Shaw

SUDOKU 1

4	5	3	7	9	6	8	2	1
1	8	9	3	5	2	6	4	7
2	7	6	4	8	1	5	9	3
9	4	2	5	7	8	1	3	6
7	6	5	1	3	9	4	8	2
8	3	1	6	2	4	9	7	5
3	2	4	9	1	5	7	6	8
6	1	7	8	4	3	2	5	9
5	9	8	2	6	7	3	1	4

CALCUDOKU 1

12x 3	4	0- 2	1
2÷ 2	1	3	1- 4
1	2÷ 2	4	3
4 4	3x 3	1	2 2

FUTOSHIKI 1

4	1	5	2	3
1	3	4	5	2
5	2	1	3	4
2	4	3	1	5
3	5	2	4	1

LOGIC PUZZLE 1 NEW KITTENS IN THE NEIGHBORHOOD

Fluffy, calico, Johns family

Rascal, black, Johnson family

Mr. Whiskers, gray, Jeffries family

Twinkie, gray-and-white, Janney family

CHAPTER 2 SOLUTIONS

CROSSWORD 2

A	C	E	D		A	S	C	O	T		S	A	R	A
B	O	N	O		C	I	R	C	E		T	R	I	M
E	A	S	Y	S	T	R	E	E	T		R	E	P	O
E	T	H	E	R	S		M	A	O		O	N	E	R
			R	N	A		P	E	N	N	Y	L	A	N	E
F	L	O	S	S	E	R			S	A	L			
E	A	U			S	O	N	S		L	E	M	O	N
M	I	D	D	L	E	O	F	T	H	E	R	O	A	D
A	T	S	E	A		F	L	A	B		M	F	A	
			P	I	P		T	O	P	L	E	S	S	
L	I	N	E	D	R	I	V	E		E	I	N		
O	D	I	N		O	N	A		F	E	T	T	L	E
R	E	E	D		P	A	P	E	R	T	R	A	I	L
D	A	C	E		E	N	E	M	Y		E	R	O	S
S	L	E	D		R	E	S	U	E		S	Y	N	E

CROSSWORD 3

R	E	P	S		A	B	L	E		S	O	F	A
E	X	I	T	S		R	E	I	N		I	C	O	N
C	O	L	I	C		L	A	N	D		D	A	R	T
I	T	S	N	O	W	O	R	N	E	V	E	R		
T	I	N	G	L	E		H	E	R	E	W	I	T	H
A	C	E		D	E	B	U	T		R	A	N	E	E
L	A	R	S		N	A	G		I	S	L	A	N	D
			P	A	I	D		A	M	O	K			
A	W	H	I	L	E		N	I	P		S	E	L	L
V	O	I	C	E		A	U	R	A	L		P	E	A
I	N	T	E	R	E	S	T		L	A	S	H	E	S
		C	R	O	S	S	T	R	A	I	N	E	R	S
D	O	H	A		T	I	R	E		R	A	D	I	O
A	V	E	C		O	S	E	S		S	P	R	E	E
M	A	S	K		P	I	E	T		S	A	R	S	

CROSSWORD 4

S	E	R	I	F		O	P	I	U	M		M	O	A
A	R	E	N	A		F	U	S	S	Y		A	R	M
F	R	E	N	C	H	F	R	I	E	S		R	I	O
E	S	L		T	A	I	L	S		T	U	G	O	N
			S	O	W	S		A	I	R	I	N	G	
E	N	G	L	I	S	H	M	U	F	F	I	N		
D	E	R	I	D	E		A	F	L	Y		A	P	E
A	R	U	T		B	R	O		S	L	I	D		
M	O	M		B	O	A	S		M	O	O	I	N	G
	P	O	L	I	S	H	S	A	U	S	A	G	E	
S	P	I	R	A	L		I	N	T	O				
T	O	N	E	R		C	A	C	T	I		A	N	A
I	R	E		I	T	A	L	I	A	N	I	C	E	S
L	E	S		N	E	P	A	L		G	R	A	S	P
E	D	S		G	L	O	R	Y		S	K	I	T	S

1950s Trivia Challenge answers: Adlai Stevenson – Chevy, with 13 million cars sold, compared with Ford's 12 million

CROSSWORD 5

E	T	N	A		B	O	T	S		O	M	A	H	A
T	H	A	I		U	T	A	H		F	I	L	E	S
H	E	A	R	T	L	I	N	E		F	L	I	R	T
A	R	C		E	L	S		I	C	E	D	T	E	A
N	E	P	A	L		A	L	O	N	E				
		C	L	U	B	S	A	N	D	W	I	C	H	
B	A	N	E		S	I	C			E	S	S	A	Y
A	C	A		R	E	O	R	D	E	R		L	I	P
L	A	S	S	O		I	N	S		P	A	N	E	
D	I	A	M	O	N	D	B	A	C	K	S			
		A	M	O	R	E		L	A	S	E	R		
D	E	C	L	I	N	E		P	I	E		T	R	A
A	D	E	L	E		S	P	A	D	E	W	O	R	K
D	A	R	E	S		S	E	R	E		A	L	E	E
S	M	A	R	T		Y	A	K	S		R	E	D	S

CROSSWORD 6

I	F	S	O		S	E	E	R		D	E	G	A	S
T	A	U	T		Y	O	Y	O		E	R	U	P	T
S	U	N	T	A	N	N	E	D		L	I	S	T	S
A	N	N	E	X	E	S		E	P	I	C			
	S	I	R	I		S	O	U	L		D	T	S	
		S	O	M	M	E		L	A	Y	O	U	T	
A	E	R		M	O	U	N	T	S	H	A	S	T	A
S	T	E	T		O	M	A	H	A		M	E	E	T
T	H	E	M	U	N	S	T	E	R	S		S	E	E
	R	E	F	I	L	L		E	A	S	E	D		
A	R	S		Y	I	P	S			W	E	E	D	
	I	S	T	O		A	G	E	N	D	A	S		
S	E	E	M	S		M	I	X	E	D	N	U	T	S
A	L	G	A	E		E	D	E	N		I	C	E	T
G	L	O	M	S		S	I	D	E		S	E	R	S

CROSSWORD 7

A	M	A	S	S		H	I	H	A	T		L	C	D
M	O	T	E	L		O	P	E	R	A		A	H	I
U	L	T	R	A	V	I	O	L	E	T		V	E	X
S	I	E	S	T	A		M	I	S	S	E	D		
E	N	S		E	L	E	V	E	N		A	N	D	A
S	E	T	A		E	D	I	T		S	U	D	A	N
		L	A	N	G	E		E	A	T	E	R	Y	
	A	L	I	C	E	W	A	L	K	E	R			
E	L	M	O	R	E		E	R	A	S	E			
R	E	E	V	E		P	R	E	T		D	O	E	S
R	A	T	E		F	O	S	S	I	L		S	T	P
	T	H	R	A	L	L		O	A	K	I	E	R	
T	H	Y		B	O	Y	S	E	N	B	E	R	R	Y
R	E	S		R	E	P	E	L		O	P	I	N	E
A	R	T		A	S	S	A	Y		R	I	S	E	R

1960s Trivia Challenge answers: Andy Griffith – Apollo 11

WORD SEARCH 2

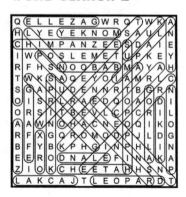

WORD SEARCH 3

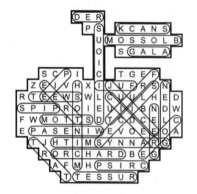

WORD SEARCH 4

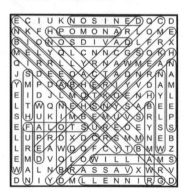

WORD SEARCH 5

WORD SEARCH 6

WORD SEARCH 7

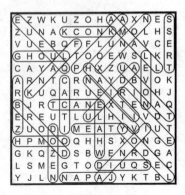

CRYPTOGRAM 2

SORTING FOLKS OUT

There are basically two types of people. People who accomplish things, and people who claim to have accomplished things. The first group is less crowded.

—Mark Twain

CRYPTOGRAM 3

IT'S OKAY TO DREAM BIG

If you have built castles in the air, your work need not be lost; that is where they should be. Now put the foundations under them.

—Henry David Thoreau

CRYPTOGRAM 4

SOME FORTITUDE NEEDED HERE

All of us have moments in our lives that test our courage. Taking children into a house with a white carpet is one of them.

—Erma Bombeck

CRYPTOGRAM 5

EVERYBODY CONTRIBUTES

The world is moved along, not only by the mighty shoves of its heroes, but also by the aggregate of tiny pushes of each honest worker.

—Helen Keller

CRYPTOGRAM 6

A SCIENCE THAT IS INHERENTLY IFFY

As far as the laws of mathematics refer to reality, they are not certain; and as far as they are certain, they do not refer to reality.

—Albert Einstein

CRYPTOGRAM 7

OFFSETTING GIFTS

Imagination was given to humans to compensate them for what they are not; a sense of humor to console them for what they are.

—Francis Bacon

SUDOKU 2

2	1	3	9	7	8	6	4	5
5	8	4	1	6	3	9	2	7
9	6	7	5	4	2	1	3	8
1	5	2	4	3	9	7	8	6
6	4	9	8	1	7	3	5	2
7	3	8	6	2	5	4	9	1
4	2	5	7	9	6	8	1	3
3	9	6	2	8	1	5	7	4
8	7	1	3	5	4	2	6	9

SUDOKU 3

9	1	5	2	4	6	8	3	7
8	7	4	1	5	3	9	2	6
6	3	2	8	7	9	4	5	1
4	9	7	3	8	2	1	6	5
1	8	6	5	9	7	3	4	2
2	5	3	6	1	4	7	9	8
7	2	9	4	6	8	5	1	3
3	4	1	7	2	5	6	8	9
5	6	8	9	3	1	2	7	4

SUDOKU 4

5	6	1	3	4	9	8	7	2
3	7	8	5	2	1	9	6	4
2	9	4	6	8	7	3	1	5
7	8	2	9	3	6	5	4	1
4	5	9	7	1	2	6	8	3
6	1	3	4	5	8	7	2	9
9	2	7	1	6	5	4	3	8
8	3	5	2	7	4	1	9	6
1	4	6	8	9	3	2	5	7

SUDOKU 5

9	8	5	1	4	3	2	7	6
3	7	4	6	5	2	8	1	9
1	2	6	8	7	9	5	3	4
4	3	2	7	1	8	6	9	5
5	6	1	2	9	4	3	8	7
7	9	8	5	3	6	1	4	2
2	4	7	3	6	1	9	5	8
6	5	3	9	8	7	4	2	1
8	1	9	4	2	5	7	6	3

SUDOKU 6

9	8	4	1	3	2	7	5	6
7	1	6	8	5	9	3	4	2
2	3	5	6	7	4	1	8	9
6	2	8	3	1	5	9	7	4
4	5	9	7	2	6	8	1	3
1	7	3	9	4	8	2	6	5
3	6	2	5	8	1	4	9	7
8	9	7	4	6	3	5	2	1
5	4	1	2	9	7	6	3	8

SUDOKU 7

6	8	4	2	5	7	3	1	9
5	9	1	6	4	3	8	2	7
3	2	7	1	8	9	4	5	6
2	1	5	8	7	4	6	9	3
8	7	6	3	9	1	2	4	5
4	3	9	5	2	6	1	7	8
9	6	2	7	1	8	5	3	4
1	4	8	9	3	5	7	6	2
7	5	3	4	6	2	9	8	1

CALCUDOKU 2

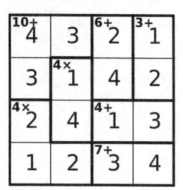

10+ 4	3	6+ 2	3+ 1
3	4x 1	4	2
4x 2	4	4+ 1	3
1	2	7+ 3	4

CALCUDOKU 3

10x 2	5	5+ 1	4	12x 3
5x 5	1	24x 2	3	4
5+ 1	1- 3	4	7+ 5	2
4	2	3 3	10x 1	5
7+ 3	4	5 5	2	1 1

CALCUDOKU 4

2x 2	1	2- 3	20x 4	5
1 1	4 4	5	2- 3	1- 2
9+ 4	6+ 2	1	5	3
5	3	6+ 4	1- 2	1 1
2- 3	5	2	1	4

CALCUDOKU 5

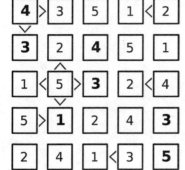

13+ 5	3 3	3- 1	4	2 2
3	5	1- 4	3- 2	5+ 1
4x 1	2÷ 2	3	5	4
4	1	5+ 2	3	2- 5
2÷ 2	4	5x 5	1	3

CALCUDOKU 6

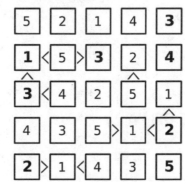

8x 4	8+ 1	3	1- 2	6+ 5
2	4	20x 5	3	1
5 5	10x 2	4	5+ 1	1- 3
3 3	5	6x 1	4	2
1 1	3	2	1- 5	4

CALCUDOKU 7

7+ 4	3	11+ 5	6	10x 1	2
6x 1	6	7+ 4	3	2 2	5
11+ 5	7+ 4	2	6x 1	8+ 3	6 6
6	1	3	2	5	4 4
5+ 3	2	7+ 6	19+ 4	5	3x 1
10x 2	5	1	4	6	3

FUTOSHIKI 2

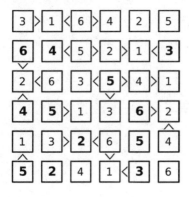

4	3	5	1	2
3	2	4	5	1
1	5	3	2	4
5	1	2	4	3
2	4	1	3	5

FUTOSHIKI 3

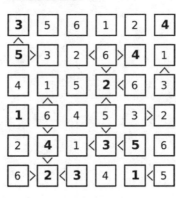

5	2	1	4	3
1	5	3	2	4
3	4	2	5	1
4	3	5	1	2
2	1	4	3	5

FUTOSHIKI 4

1	2	5	3	4
5	1	2	4	3
4	3	1	5	2
3	5	4	2	1
2	4	3	1	5

FUTOSHIKI 5

3	1	6	4	2	5
6	4	5	2	1	3
2	6	3	5	4	1
4	5	1	3	6	2
1	3	2	6	5	4
5	2	4	1	3	6

FUTOSHIKI 6

3	5	6	1	2	4
5	3	2	6	4	1
4	1	5	2	6	3
1	6	4	5	3	2
2	4	1	3	5	6
6	2	3	4	1	5

FUTOSHIKI 7

5	2	6	4	1	3
6	5	2	3	4	1
1	6	5	2	3	4
3	4	1	5	2	6
4	1	3	6	5	2
2	3	4	1	6	5

LOGIC PUZZLE 2 CONSIGNMENTS IN AT ART'S GALLERY

Cynthia Studio, watercolors, $600–$1,500
David Daring, oil-on-canvas still lifes, $2,000–$3,000
Evan Aesthete, mixed-media abstracts, $500–$1,000
Pamela Primo, sculptures, $1,500–$2,500

LOGIC PUZZLE 3 THE FISHING COMPETITION

Fred, 14.59 lb., 4.08 lb.
Ian, 15.17 lb., 4.85 lb. (winner)
Steve, 14.11 lb., 4.23 lb.
Hank, 15.34 lb. (winner), 4.52 lb.

LOGIC PUZZLE 4 OFFICE SPACE

Smith & Jackson, CPAs, 3rd floor, 2,000 sq. ft.
Peerless Empl. Svc., 1st floor, 1,300 sq. ft.
Edelsten Ins. Agcy., 2nd floor, 1,000 sq. ft.
Jackson & Smith law firm, 4th floor, 1,600 sq. ft.

LOGIC PUZZLE 5 FURNITURE DELIVERY

Sectional, $1,895, dark gray
Sofa bed, $1,995, beige
Traditional, $2,095, light gray
Victorian, $2,300, blue

LOGIC PUZZLE 6 FREIGHT TRAINS

1st, 55 stack cars, 14 reefers
2nd, 60 stack cars, 18 reefers
3rd, 68 stack cars, 12 reefers
4th, 65 stack cars, 6 reefers

CHAPTER 3 SOLUTIONS

CROSSWORD 8

```
B U T L E R ■ O N C E ■ B A T
A S H O R E ■ N E O N ■ A R I
H E A D O F S T A T E ■ R E E
■ D I E D ■ H I R E ■ P E A R
■ ■ S E S A M E ■ S O N ■ ■ ■
S W A T ■ C H E S T E R T O N
M A R A C A S ■ T A D ■ S P A
A S T R A L ■ L E A S E S ■ ■
C O D ■ L E I ■ T O R M E N T
K N E E L S D O W N ■ E A S Y
■ ■ A B S ■ A R I S E N ■ ■ ■
B U L B ■ C H A S ■ V A V A
A T E ■ F O O T T H E B I L L
B A R ■ B R A E ■ I N L E T S
A H S ■ I N N S ■ S T E W E D
```

CROSSWORD 9

```
A D E L E ■ E R A S ■ R A M P
D E V O S ■ T O T O ■ E W E R
I S A A C ■ H O O T ■ E R G O
N I N T H S Y M P H O N Y ■ ■
■ ■ H E E L S ■ E P A ■ ■ ■ ■
T H R E A T ■ E R E C T E D
H E E ■ T H I R D E S T A T E
O L A F ■ M E N ■ S P A N ■ ■
S E C O N D P L A C E ■ E I N
E N T R E E S ■ H A R D L Y
■ E A N ■ T I A R A ■ ■ ■ ■
■ U M P T E E N T H T I M E
C A P O ■ I R A S ■ A T S E A
A D O S ■ S I R E ■ R E L E T
W A N T ■ T E S T ■ T R E K S
```

1970s Trivia Challenge answers: Concorde – *Bohemian Rhapsody*

CROSSWORD 10

```
S P A ■ S C U B A ■ P S S T S
K O I ■ A E S O P ■ A L P H A
I L L ■ B L O O P E R R E E L
L E E S ■ S K I R T ■ N O T
L A R I A T ■ M A S S A C R E
E X O R B I T A N T ■ D E E R
D E N ■ O N I N ■ T E R M S
■ ■ ■ A U T O ■ A M O S ■ ■
S M A R T ■ O M E N ■ T S E
T A N G ■ S P R I N G B O K S
E S T O P P E D ■ D A R N I T
P O E ■ E A T E N ■ A N N E
I N N E R C I R C L E ■ A N E
N I N E S ■ T E A L S ■ G E M
S C A R E ■ E D A M S ■ E R S
```

CROSSWORD 11

```
P A S H A ■ S L E D ■ I S L E
S T O O L ■ P O K E ■ N E A R
H A R D D R I V E S ■ T A D A
A R E ■ ■ O N E ■ C L O S E T
W I N S O M E ■ H E A T H ■ ■
■ ■ C A P T A I N H O O K S
F L O A T S ■ L S D ■ R N A
L O U T S ■ G I S ■ E P E E S
A G T ■ R O B ■ A R I S E S
B Y E B Y E B I R D I E ■ ■
■ ■ R E I N S ■ E V E R E S T
E R M I N E ■ A E I ■ R T E
M O O G ■ W A F F L E I R O N
M U S E ■ A B E E ■ S P O R T
A T T S ■ L E W D ■ P A R K S
```

CROSSWORD 12

```
T A M E ■ A S P E N ■ D A D O
A P E X ■ M E A R A ■ A S I F
R A Y C H A R L E S ■ I S N T
P R E L A T E ■ A L L E G E
S T R U T ■ N E I L S I M O N
■ ■ D E P E N D ■ D E B ■ ■
A M P E R E ■ S O T ■ S L E W
B O A ■ S T A N L E E ■ E G O
C O R E ■ E R A ■ S L E D G E
■ ■ A N A ■ G R A H A M ■ ■
B I L L Y J O E L ■ T U L S A
O N L I N E ■ A T E L I E R
O D E S ■ L A R R Y D A V I D
T I L T ■ L A Y U P ■ T I N E
H E S S ■ S H A M E ■ E D E N
```

1980s Trivia Challenge answers: Margaret Thatcher – *Back to the Future*

CROSSWORD 13

```
F A S T S ■ E B B ■ I H O P S
U L T R A ■ A L E ■ N E W E R
S P O I L ■ R O E ■ F A N T A
S H O O T I N G S T A R ■ ■
Y A P ■ I D S ■ E N T A I L
■ ■ L E I ■ A I N T ■ I N A
A S T E R O I D S ■ A B O U T
S T E W ■ T A I N T ■ A L I T
T E N D S ■ M E T E O R I T E
I V E ■ T A B U ■ A P E ■ ■
R E T O R T ■ T R A ■ A M S
■ ■ H A L L E Y S C O M E T
O C E A N ■ A R I ■ I R O N Y
H O A R D ■ T I N ■ T E N S E
M O R E S ■ E N G ■ Y O G A S
```

CROSSWORD 14

```
A N I N ■ S A G A ■ A B H O R
I O N A ■ A I N T ■ D R I L L
M I K E T R O U T ■ V A S E S
I D I ■ O I L ■ F E S T ■ ■
N E E D S ■ I N N E R S O L E
G A R I S H ■ I A M B ■ R E M
■ ■ N E O ■ P T A ■ L I E U
J A C K S O N P O L L O C K S
A L A S ■ K O I ■ E A T ■ ■
I S L ■ P A T E ■ S H U T U P
L O A N S H A R K ■ O S A K A
■ M A A S ■ E A R ■ M A R
S N A R L ■ L A N C E B A S S
H A R E M ■ A I D E ■ A L E E
A M I S S ■ C L O D ■ M E S S
```

WORD SEARCH 8

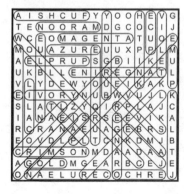

WORD SEARCH 9

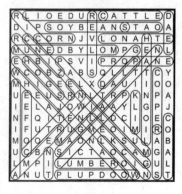

WORD SEARCH 10

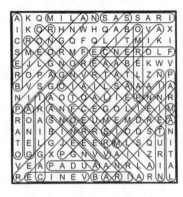

WORD SEARCH 11

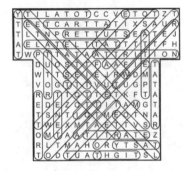

WORD SEARCH 12

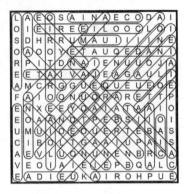

WORD SEARCH 13

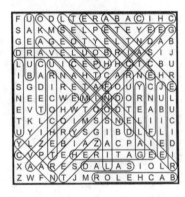

WORD SEARCH 14

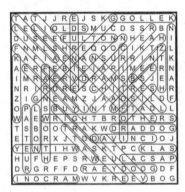

CRYPTOGRAM 8

CONTRADICTION

Humans are rational animals who always lose their tempers when they are called upon to act in accordance with the dictates of reason.

—Oscar Wilde

CRYPTOGRAM 9

THE SOURCE OF BRILLIANCE

Neither a lofty degree of intelligence nor imagination nor both together go to the making of genius. Love, love, love, that is the soul of genius.

—Wolfgang Amadeus Mozart

CRYPTOGRAM 10

DESTINY CALLED

My mother said to me, "If you are a soldier, you will become a general. If you are a monk, you will become the Pope." Instead, I was a painter, and became Picasso.

—Pablo Picasso

CRYPTOGRAM 11

A LITTLE HUMILITY IS IN ORDER

When you get to be President, there are all those things, the honors, the twenty-one gun salutes, all those things. You have to remember it isn't for you, it's for the Presidency.

—Harry S. Truman

CHAPTER 3 SOLUTIONS, CONT.

CRYPTOGRAM 12

DISTINGUISHING CHARACTERISTIC

The whole difference between construction and creation is exactly this: that a thing constructed can only be loved after it is constructed; but a thing created is loved before it exists.

—Charles Dickens

CRYPTOGRAM 13

THE VALUE OF SHARED MIRTH

One hearty laugh together will bring enemies into a closer communion of heart than hours spent on both sides in inward wrestling with the mental demon of uncharitable feeling.

—William James

SUDOKU 8

3	9	4	1	6	2	8	5	7
6	5	7	4	8	9	3	2	1
2	1	8	7	3	5	6	9	4
5	7	6	8	1	4	9	3	2
1	3	9	5	2	6	4	7	8
4	8	2	9	7	3	1	6	5
8	6	3	2	4	7	5	1	9
9	2	1	3	5	8	7	4	6
7	4	5	6	9	1	2	8	3

SUDOKU 9

5	6	8	1	4	3	7	2	9
4	2	1	9	7	8	3	5	6
3	9	7	5	6	2	1	4	8
8	3	9	7	2	5	4	6	1
1	4	2	6	3	9	5	8	7
6	7	5	4	8	1	2	9	3
9	8	3	2	5	7	6	1	4
7	5	6	8	1	4	9	3	2
2	1	4	3	9	6	8	7	5

SUDOKU 10

8	6	4	1	5	9	7	2	3
3	5	9	2	4	7	1	6	8
2	1	7	8	3	6	4	5	9
7	4	3	5	6	2	9	8	1
6	9	5	4	1	8	2	3	7
1	2	8	7	9	3	6	4	5
9	7	6	3	8	4	5	1	2
4	3	1	9	2	5	8	7	6
5	8	2	6	7	1	3	9	4

SUDOKU 11

2	8	1	5	7	6	3	4	9
4	7	5	9	2	3	1	8	6
6	9	3	4	1	8	5	7	2
7	5	2	1	6	9	4	3	8
3	4	8	7	5	2	9	6	1
9	1	6	3	8	4	7	2	5
5	6	4	8	3	1	2	9	7
1	2	9	6	4	7	8	5	3
8	3	7	2	9	5	6	1	4

SUDOKU 12

2	5	9	7	4	1	8	3	6
7	6	3	5	9	8	1	4	2
4	8	1	2	3	6	5	9	7
9	7	8	1	5	3	2	6	4
5	4	2	6	8	7	3	1	9
1	3	6	4	2	9	7	5	8
8	1	5	9	6	2	4	7	3
3	9	7	8	1	4	6	2	5
6	2	4	3	7	5	9	8	1

SUDOKU 13

7	8	1	6	9	2	3	4	5
9	5	2	4	7	3	6	1	8
3	6	4	8	1	5	2	7	9
4	2	7	9	6	8	5	3	1
1	3	6	2	5	7	8	9	4
8	9	5	1	3	4	7	6	2
5	1	9	3	2	6	4	8	7
6	7	8	5	4	1	9	2	3
2	4	3	7	8	9	1	5	6

SUDOKU 14

7	2	3	9	5	6	8	4	1
5	4	6	8	2	1	7	9	3
9	8	1	7	3	4	2	6	5
6	5	4	2	8	3	1	7	9
2	7	9	4	1	5	3	8	6
1	3	8	6	7	9	4	5	2
8	9	5	3	4	2	6	1	7
4	6	2	1	9	7	5	3	8
3	1	7	5	6	8	9	2	4

CHAPTER 3 SOLUTIONS, CONT.

SUDOKU 15

5	4	9	6	2	1	7	8	3
2	7	8	5	9	3	6	4	1
6	3	1	4	8	7	2	9	5
4	2	7	9	3	6	5	1	8
8	1	3	7	5	2	4	6	9
9	6	5	8	1	4	3	2	7
3	9	4	1	6	5	8	7	2
1	5	6	2	7	8	9	3	4
7	8	2	3	4	9	1	5	6

CALCUDOKU 8

6	2	4	5	3	1
2	6	1	4	5	3
5	3	2	1	6	4
4	5	3	6	1	2
3	1	6	2	4	5
1	4	5	3	2	6

CALCUDOKU 9

3	4	6	1	2	5
5	2	4	3	6	1
6	1	3	5	4	2
1	3	2	6	5	4
2	6	5	4	1	3
4	5	1	2	3	6

CALCUDOKU 10

4	5	3	6	1	2
2	6	1	4	3	5
6	2	5	3	4	1
1	4	2	5	6	3
3	1	4	2	5	6
5	3	6	1	2	4

CALCUDOKU 11

1	2	5	6	3	4
5	6	4	1	2	3
4	5	1	3	6	2
3	4	2	5	1	6
2	3	6	4	5	1
6	1	3	2	4	5

CALCUDOKU 12

2	6	1	4	3	5
5	2	4	3	1	6
1	5	6	2	4	3
6	3	2	1	5	4
3	4	5	6	2	1
4	1	3	5	6	2

CALCUDOKU 13

1	6	2	3	4	5
4	5	6	1	2	3
2	1	5	6	3	4
3	4	1	5	6	2
6	3	4	2	5	1
5	2	3	4	1	6

FUTOSHIKI 8

1	3	**2** <	5	4
4	1	5	**2** <	3
3 <	**5**	1	4	2
2	4 >	3	1	5
5	2	4	3 >	1

FUTOSHIKI 9

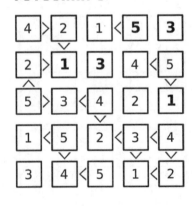

4 >	2	1 <	**5**	**3**
2 >	**1**	**3**	4 <	5
5 >	3 <	4	2	**1**
1 <	5	2 <	3	4
3	4 <	5	1 <	2

FUTOSHIKI 10

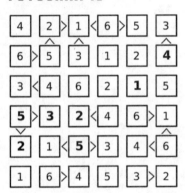

FUTOSHIKI 11

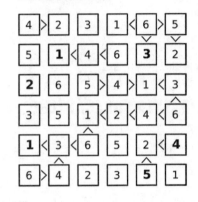

FUTOSHIKI 12

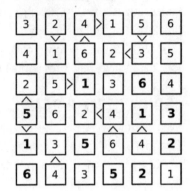

FUTOSHIKI 13

LOGIC PUZZLE 7 MIKE, THE AUTO MECHANIC
Janice, 2020 Chevy, 30,000 mi. service, 1st
Jim, 2018 Ford, reline brakes, 3rd
John, 2019 Subaru, resolve "check engine" light, 2nd
Joe, 2016 Volvo, new tires and wheel alignment, 4th

LOGIC PUZZLE 8 RATING WEATHER FORECASTERS
WeatherInfo.com, 91 deg. (1), 12 mph (1), ⅓ inch (2)
Channel 2, 89 deg. (3), 10 mph (2), ½ inch (3)
KGXZ Radio, 90 deg. (2), 8 mph (3), ¼ inch (1)
FWS, 93 deg., 15 mph, ⅛ inch
(The number in parentheses beside each forecast ranks the forecast in relation to how close it is to the FWS figure.)

LOGIC PUZZLE 9 BIRD-WATCHING
Bernie, 19 species, 4 cardinals, 7 robins
Bert, 25 species, 2 cardinals, 3 robins
Bonnie, 15 species, 3 cardinals, 4 robins
Brenda, 21 species, 5 cardinals, 6 robins

LOGIC PUZZLE 10 THE HOT DOG CART
Ball fields, $400 hot dogs, $210 snacks, $350 soft drinks, $960 total (best location)
Busy roads, $310 hot dogs, $250 snacks, $300 soft drinks, $860 total
Boat dock, $340 hot dogs, $170 snacks, $310 soft drinks, $820 total
Zoo, $370 hot dogs, $190 snacks, $330 soft drinks, $890 total

LOGIC PUZZLE 11 SPRUCING UP THE STREET
1802 Shady Ln., 2-story colonial, paint, picket fence
1804 Shady Ln., rambler, roof, landscaping
1807 Shady Ln., split-level, encl. porch, driveway
1815 Shady Ln., cottage, windows, swimming pool

LOGIC PUZZLE 12 BUSY AFTERNOON AT THE AIRPORT
3:00 to 3:30, 1 4-engine, 6 2-engines, 2 prop planes
3:30 to 4:00, 0 4-engines, 5 2-engines, 4 prop planes
4:00 to 4:30, 2 4-engines, 4 2-engines, 3 prop planes
4:30 to 5:00, 3 4-engines, 8 2-engines, 1 prop plane

CHAPTER 4 SOLUTIONS

CROSSWORD 15

```
O P T   D E A L     G O B I
R E O   R O N D O   R I V E R
C A R G O H O L D   E N E R O
A S T R O   S I G M A   R I N
    I T D   B E R M U D A
C O U N S E L   T E A R
A L P S   N A S T   R E A P S
R E I   S Y M B O L S   F L U
D O N U T   P A L E   S T O P
    T M A N   D I G E S T S
☆ C H A M B E R   F R A
L I E   M A R A T   E M I T S
E R A S E   I N E L A S T I C
T R I E R   E G R E T   E R A
S I R E   S E M I ○ M E T
```

1990s Trivia Challenge answers: Madeleine Albright – *Titanic*

CROSSWORD 16

```
S P L A T   C L E A R   C R U
I R I S H   H I N G E   R E T
N I C K E L O D E O N   E S T
A C E   E I O   E L O P E
T I N S T A R   S T E E L E R
R E S H I P   S H O   D E L L
A R E A L   J E A N S   S L Y
    M E T A L L I C A
B I B   R U P E E   A L I S T
I S E E   B A S   B L A N K S
G O L D M A N   B R A S S I E
S T A T E   A R E   H D T
H O T   C O P P E R H E A D S
O P E   C L O S E   T E P E E
T E D   A D D E D   S E E D S
```

CROSSWORD 17

```
S I N G   S H A H   G L A D E
O R E O   P A L O   A I R E R
D O U B T I N G T O M M A S O
A N T L E R S   D R U B B E D
    I S A   R O B T   I R E
S A I N T L U I G I   B A T S
O R O   A S T A   T A R N
P I N O T   E L I   R O S E S
    O N E S   T R A C   E A T
I S S O   P O O R C H I A R A
N A P   P I U S   C A N
A T H E A R T   R E I N S I N
P I E T R O P R I N C I P L E
E R R O R   U N I T   N A S T
T E E N Y   T A S S   G R A S
```

CROSSWORD 18

```
S P A M   C C S   P H A S E S
A R I A   A A U   L A M E N T
W O R K P E R M   U G A N D A
    E A S I E S T   N O U N
U K E   L A B R E A T A R P S
L A D D E R   E R R S
T R E Y   N O N C E   H U E
R E M E M B E R T H E T A N S
A N A   B U C K O   A R C S
    E A S T   S A M P L E
P R O F S H A R I N G   Y E N
L E I F   I R O N I N G
O F L A T E   C U T I T O U T
P I E C E S   H I C   O R S O
S T R E E T   E T H   S E A T
```

CROSSWORD 19

```
T O N G A   S P A T E   T N T
A C O R N   E L T O N   R O W
K A R A T E C O O P S   A G O
E L A N   V O W   B U E N O S
S A D D L E   B E R E T S
    M A R C O M A D N E S S
S T O A T   L Y E S   A C H E
U H F   E T O   T S P   T O E
R A F T   A U D I   E S S E N
F I R E S I D E C O A T
    O R E L S E   P L A T T E
S C A R A B   P R E   M A A S
H O D   W O O S O N F I R S T
A V E   A N D E S   E N O T E
H E R   Y E A T S   W A T E R
```

2000s Trivia Challenge answers: 2007 – *The Office*

CROSSWORD 20

```
A H A S   M I C   A B B E S S
P A S A D E N A   M I L D E W
A L A B A M A N   E N T I R E
R E D I R E C T I N G   T E E
T R A N E   T E A S   F O N T
    S W I R L   F O R G E
M I S S   H O B   O B R I E N
A N T E P E N U L T I M A T E
S T A T I N   R O T   S L I D
S U I T E   S Y N O D
M I R O   P A T E   E N U R E
E T C   B R E A S T B O N E S
D I A B L O   L O W T I D E S
I N S E A M   E M I S S I V E
A G E N T S   S E N   E D E N
```

WORD SEARCH 15

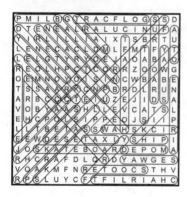

WORD SEARCH 16

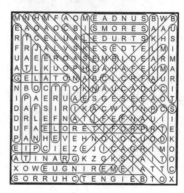

WORD SEARCH 17

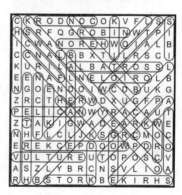

WORD SEARCH 18

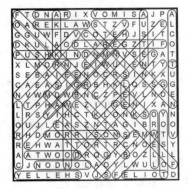

WORD SEARCH 19

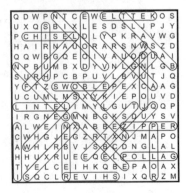

WORD SEARCH 20

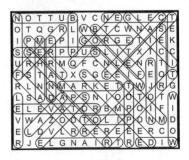

CRYPTOGRAM 14

DON'T BE COWED

We gain strength, and courage, and confidence by each experience in which we really stop to look fear in the face … we must do that which we think we cannot do.

—Eleanor Roosevelt

CRYPTOGRAM 15

FORWARD-LOOKING IDEAL

The assertion that "all men are created equal" was of no practical use in effecting our separation from Great Britain and it was placed in the Declaration not for that, but for future use.

—Abraham Lincoln

CRYPTOGRAM 16

THE AUTHOR'S PRODUCT

Every reader finds himself. The writer's work is merely a kind of optical instrument that make it possible for the reader to discern what, without this book, he would perhaps never have seen in himself.

—Marcel Proust

CRYPTOGRAM 17

THE MAGIC OF THE WOODS

It is not so much for its beauty that the forest makes a claim upon people's hearts, as for that subtle something, that quality of air, that emanation from old trees, that so wonderfully changes and renews a weary spirit.

—Robert Louis Stevenson

CRYPTOGRAM 18

MORE ISN'T ALWAYS BETTER

As the biggest library, if it is in disorder, is not as useful as a small but well-arranged one, so you may accumulate a vast amount of knowledge but it will be of far less value than a much smaller amount if you have not thought it over for yourself.

—Arthur Schopenhauer

CRYPTOGRAM 19

MERCY, THE HIGHEST VIRTUE

Let us not listen to those who think we ought to be angry with our enemies, and who believe this to be great and manly. Nothing is so praiseworthy, nothing so clearly shows a great and noble soul, as clemency and readiness to forgive.

—Cicero

SUDOKU 16

1	3	2	8	4	7	5	9	6
9	6	4	3	2	5	7	8	1
7	5	8	9	6	1	4	3	2
8	2	1	4	7	6	3	5	9
6	7	3	5	9	8	2	1	4
5	4	9	1	3	2	8	6	7
4	1	6	7	5	3	9	2	8
2	9	5	6	8	4	1	7	3
3	8	7	2	1	9	6	4	5

SUDOKU 17

2	6	9	7	3	1	4	8	5
1	4	7	8	2	5	9	3	6
3	8	5	4	6	9	1	7	2
9	3	8	6	7	4	2	5	1
5	1	2	3	9	8	7	6	4
6	7	4	5	1	2	3	9	8
7	2	3	1	5	6	8	4	9
4	9	6	2	8	3	5	1	7
8	5	1	9	4	7	6	2	3

SUDOKU 18

9	7	3	8	2	1	4	6	5
4	8	5	6	7	3	9	2	1
6	2	1	5	9	4	7	3	8
8	6	9	7	3	5	2	1	4
3	1	2	4	6	8	5	9	7
5	4	7	2	1	9	6	8	3
2	9	8	3	4	7	1	5	6
7	3	6	1	5	2	8	4	9
1	5	4	9	8	6	3	7	2

SUDOKU 19

3	1	6	4	8	2	5	7	9
5	8	4	6	7	9	1	2	3
9	7	2	1	3	5	6	8	4
7	4	5	3	9	1	2	6	8
1	9	8	2	4	6	3	5	7
2	6	3	7	5	8	9	4	1
6	5	7	9	1	4	8	3	2
8	3	9	5	2	7	4	1	6
4	2	1	8	6	3	7	9	5

SUDOKU 20

2	8	6	7	3	1	4	9	5
9	7	4	2	5	6	3	1	8
1	3	5	4	8	9	7	2	6
5	9	3	1	2	8	6	7	4
8	4	2	6	7	3	9	5	1
7	6	1	9	4	5	2	8	3
3	1	7	8	9	4	5	6	2
4	2	8	5	6	7	1	3	9
6	5	9	3	1	2	8	4	7

SUDOKU 21

9	4	1	7	8	6	5	2	3
3	6	7	9	2	5	8	4	1
5	2	8	1	3	4	7	6	9
8	5	4	3	6	7	1	9	2
2	7	6	8	1	9	3	5	4
1	3	9	4	5	2	6	7	8
7	1	2	6	9	8	4	3	5
4	8	5	2	7	3	9	1	6
6	9	3	5	4	1	2	8	7

CALCUDOKU 14

$^{1-}$1	2	$^{10+}$3	$^{9+}$4	5	^{72x}6
$^{7+}$2	5	1	6	3	4
^{4}4	^{18x}3	$^{8+}$6	2	^{4x}1	$^{6+}$5
^{15x}5	6	$^{9+}$2	3	4	1
3	^{1}1	4	^{30x}5	6	^{2}2
$^{2-}$6	4	^{5}5	1	$^{1-}$2	3

CALCUDOKU 15

$^{8+}$2	$^{0-}$4	6	$^{2-}$5	$^{4+}$3	1
6	2	$^{3+}$1	3	^{24x}4	$^{9+}$5
$^{11+}$5	3	2	6	1	4
3	$^{13+}$1	4	^{60x}2	5	6
^{4x}4	5	3	1	$^{3:}$6	2
1	$^{11+}$6	5	$^{2-}$4	2	^{3}3

CALCUDOKU 16

$^{10+}$2	3	$^{5+}$4	1	$^{1-}$6	5
5	^{30x}6	$^{5+}$2	$^{13+}$4	3	$^{2:}$1
$^{7+}$4	5	3	6	$^{3-}$1	2
3	^{60x}1	5	$^{5+}$2	4	$^{10+}$6
$^{6:}$1	2	6	3	$^{3-}$5	4
6	^{20x}4	1	5	2	^{3}3

CHAPTER 4 SOLUTIONS, CONT.

CALCUDOKU 17

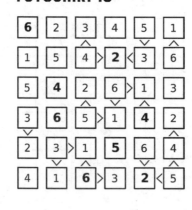

8+5	3	8+4	1	4-6	2:2
4x4	8+6	3	17+5	2	1
1	2	7+6	4	5	3-3
14+2	5	1	3	4:4	6
3	4	2-2	6	1	1-5
5-6	1	5	2	3	4

CALCUDOKU 18

9+6	2x1	2	1-3	5	10+4
2	9+5	4	1	6x3	6
1	24x4	6	10x5	2	8+3
12x3	2:6	1	2	4x4	5
4	3	14+5	6	1	2x2
7+5	2	3	2-4	6	1

CALCUDOKU 19

6+2	3	1	9+5	4	30x6
30x6	24x2	4	2-3	1	5
5	80x4	3	5-1	6	2-2
1	5	14+6	6x2	3	4
4	5-1	2	6	30x5	3
3	6	1-5	4	2	1

FUTOSHIKI 14

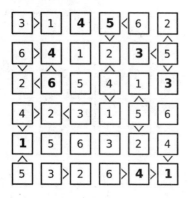

6	5	3	1	**4**	2
1	6	2	**5**	**3**	4
5	**4**	**1**	2	6	**3**
2	1	4	3	5	6
3	2	6	4	1	5
4	3	**5**	6	2	1

FUTOSHIKI 15

6	2	3	4	5	1
1	5	4	**2**	3	6
5	**4**	2	6	1	3
3	**6**	5	1	**4**	2
2	3	1	**5**	6	4
4	1	**6**	3	**2**	5

FUTOSHIKI 16

3	5	**1**	4	**6**	2
6	2	5	1	3	**4**
2	4	3	6	1	5
4	**3**	6	5	2	1
1	6	4	**2**	**5**	3
5	1	2	**3**	4	6

FUTOSHIKI 17

3	1	**4**	**5**	6	2
6	**4**	1	2	**3**	5
2	**6**	5	4	1	**3**
4	2	**3**	1	5	6
1	5	6	3	2	4
5	3	2	6	**4**	**1**

FUTOSHIKI 18

3	4	1	2	6	**7**	5
6	3	7	4	**5**	**1**	**2**
2	6	3	1	4	**5**	7
1	**7**	5	**6**	2	4	**3**
7	2	**4**	5	1	3	6
4	5	2	**3**	7	6	**1**
5	1	6	7	3	**2**	4

CHAPTER 4 SOLUTIONS, CONT.

LOGIC PUZZLE 13 SATURDAY'S FARMERS MARKET
Doug's, farm cheese, 170 lbs. tomatoes, 340 ears of corn
Farmer John, potpourri, 130 lbs. tomatoes, 500 ears of corn (most)
Fresh/Farm, ham/biscuits, 160 lbs. tomatoes, 440 ears of corn
Hank's, honey, 180 lbs. tomatoes, 420 ears of corn
Julie/Joe's, apple butter, 200 lbs. tomatoes (most), 400 ears of corn

LOGIC PUZZLE 14 PACIFIC ISLAND NATIONS
Fiji, 333 islands, Vita Levu, 4,026 sq. mi.
Palau, 340 islands, Babeldaob, 143 sq. mi.
Samoa, 9 islands, Savai'i, 659 sq. mi.
Solomon Isl., 992 islands, Guadalcanal, 2,047 sq. mi.
Tonga, 169 islands, Tongatapu, 101 sq. mi.
2010s Trivia Challenge answers: London – Daniel Day-Lewis

LOGIC PUZZLE 15 ICE CREAM SHOPS
1st, mall, Margo, 1,800 cones
2nd, near school, Mike, 1,650 cones
3rd, airport, Melissa, 1,850 cones
4th, waterfront, Mack, 1,700 cones
5th, downtown, Mark, 1,900 cones

LOGIC PUZZLE 16 CONTAINER SHIPS
MV ISAAC J, 5:00 PM, 6,830 inbound, 7,900 outbound
MV MARLAK, 3:00 PM, 7,900 inbound, 8,750 outbound
MV MARYSUE, 11:00 AM, 8,130 inbound, 8,110 outbound
MV PRECISION, 1:00 PM, 6,550 inbound, 5,900 outbound
MV VICEROY, 9:00 AM, 7,250 inbound, 7,400 outbound

LOGIC PUZZLE 17 RANKING THE BEST BEACHES
Boka, 4th, wide beach, rental houses
Johnsonville, 5th, shallow water, boardwalk
Orange Coast, 3rd, great waves, state park
Saturn, 2nd, white sand, pier
Southwinds, 1st, reefs, equipment shops

LOGIC PUZZLE 18 EXCITING FINISH AT THE SPEEDWAY
Steve Stocker, car No. 50, Fizzy Cola, 2nd
Phil Fleet, car No. 16, Chewy Candy Bar, 1st (winner)
Doug Draftin, car No. 27, Marvel Bread, 4th
Pete Piston, car No. 9, A+ Engine Additive, 5th
Stu Speedster, car No. 73, Acme Auto Parts, 3rd
2020s Trivia Challenge answers: *Spider Man: No Way Home* – pickleball

ACKNOWLEDGMENT

I deeply appreciate the important contribution that Patrick Min made to this book—he constructed the delightful Calcudoku and Futoshiki puzzles that are included in it. Patrick is an accomplished puzzle master and oversees the premier Calcudoku website, calcudoku.org. I heartily recommend you pay a visit to the site for more Calcudoku-solving fun.

ABOUT THE AUTHOR

Phil Fraas is a longtime constructor of crossword puzzles and an author of several puzzle books. He also oversees, and constructs puzzles for, a free crossword, Sudoku, and word search website—YourPuzzleSource.com.